1381

The Peel Affinity

An English Knight's Household
in the Fourteenth Century

A Production of
La Belle Compagnie
and friends

Principal Text: Elizabeth Johnson, Robert Charrette

Supplemental Text: Eric Johnson, Will McLean, Peter Taylor, Joann Socash

Additional Material: Erci Nolan, Deborah Peters, Stephen Bloch, Christopher Bowen, Elizabeth Bennett

Editor: Dorothy Altmiller
Readers: Meg Leene Gronvall, Katherine Johnson, Mark Shier, Barbara Gordon. Linda Taylor, Terry Taylor

Principal Photography: Robert Charrette, Joann Socash
Additional Photography: Eric Johnson, Scott Nolan, Brian Brown, Gary Halstead, Mark Shier, Dan Hill, William Grobbel, Paul Lalonde, Kate Brown, Craig Allen
Digital Manipulation: Robert Charrette, Alexander Bradley, Eric Johnson, Joann Socash

Book Design: Alexander Bradley
Maps: Peter Taylor

Published in the United States by
Shumacher Publishing LLC
1900 Sauers Rd
Harrisburg PA 17110

Acknowledgements

Special thanks to: Robert MacPherson, armorer; Marianne Hanson and Billy and Charlie's Finest Pewter Goods; Mark Shier and Gaukler Medieval Wares; Chris Bowen and Dru Shoemaker; Max Engel and Northstar Armoury; John van Hassel and Windrose Armory; Doug Strong; Brian Price; Meg Leene Gronvall (embroidery); Jennifer Johnson (special make-up); and, of course, the hardy, harried, and hardworking members of La Belle Compagnie.

Other sources of artifacts: Nicole Allen (Revival Clothing); Wade Allen, armorer; Tim Bray (Albion Woodworks); Bill Darr, bowyer; David Calafrancesco; Mike Cardiff (Magick Badger Ironworks); Del Tin Armi Antiche; Depeeka; Fred Farner, pewterer; Mike Gann (Blackwood Jewellery); Bill Grobbel; Steve Gurzler; Julie Guthrie; Jeff Hedgecock (Historic Arms and Armor); John Heinz (Herugrim, Inc.); Glenn Herbert (Gode Erthe Pottes); Highland Armouries; Impedimenta; Tom Justus; King's Keep; Gary Link (Jactance); Peter Marques (Tentsmiths); Walter McAuliffe; Laura Donnelly Morgan; Museum Replicas Limited; Northerner.com Historical Glass; Gwen Nowrick (Black Swan Designs); Doug Odom; Greg Priest-Dolman; Steve Sheldon (Forth Armouries); Karen Smith (Fettered Cock Pewterers); Talbot's Fine Accessories; Mike and Belinda Tartaglio (The Practical Goose); Daniel Weil, painter; Tim Whitcomb (StarHammer Arts Magickal); Robin Wood, turner; and a host of museum shops, re-enactment suppliers, and commercial trading operations whose products (by craftspeople unknown to us) have graced our encampments and presentations over the years.

Period pictures reproduced with the permission of: page 13 The British Library Board; page 21 Bibliuotheque Royale Albert 1er, Brussels; page 23 ; The British Library Board; page 27, left Dean and Chapter of Westminster; page 27, right: Bibliotheque Nationale de France.

Backgrounds photographed at: Weald and Downland Open Air Museum, Singleton, West Sussex, England; Middelaldercentret, Nykøbing Falster, Denmark; Barley Hall, York, England; Wine Merchant's House and city gates, Southampton, England; Mont St. Michel, Normandy, France; Ste-Chappelle, Paris, France; Tewkesbury, England; Winchester, England; the Hanse Cogge, Bremen, Germany; various Hampshire locales, England; Marietta Manor, Maryland, USA; Jamestown Settlement (Jamestown-Yorktown Foundation), Virginia, USA; Washington (DC) National Cathedral, USA; and Nolan-Stern-Nolan Studios, Virginia, USA.

Our Cast: Peter Adams, Brian Altmiller, Dorothy Altmiller, Genevieve Altmiller, Andrew Bailey, Jesse Bailey, Tim Ballew, James Barker, Charles Bennett, Elizabeth Bennett, Jessica Bethel, Jonathan Blair, Stephen Bloch, Christine Bodziak, Christopher Bowen, Alexander Bradley, Renée Camus Bradley, Andrew Breeden, Jeffrey Breeden, Susan Breeden, Thomas Breeden, Brian Brown, Robert Charrette, Bobby Charron, Gordon Clark, Karyn Clark, Madelyn Clark, Mariel Clark, Christian Clausen, Scott Cozad, Regan Dixon, Daniel Drolet, Maxwell Engel, Cal Everett, Cam Everett, Wendy Everett, Barbara Gordon, Benjamin Gronvall, Meg Leene Gronvall, Cynthia Halstead, Gary Halstead, Stephen Hick, Kimberly Hulse, Thomas Hundley, Adam Johnson, Daniel Johnson, Elizabeth Johnson, Eric Johnson, Jeffrey Johnson, Jennifer Johnson, Katherine Johnson, Marie Johnson, Michael Johnson, Patricia Johnson, Paul Johnson, Rachel Johnson, Ruth Johnson, Sheryl Johnson, Stephen Johnson, Thomas Johnson, Timothy Johnson, Davyd Jordan, James Jordan, Scott Jordan, Martin Keeley, Hugh Knight, Glen Kyle, Paul Lalonde, Andrew Lang, Walker Trent Lesan, Philip Mauro, Will McLean, Kiara Morgan, Laura Donnelly Morgan, Ashley Nolan, Erci Nolan, Scott Nolan, Steven J. Nolan, Andrea Requa, J. Philip Parsons, Greg Pearson, Deborah Peters, Katelyn Peters, Jennifer Povey, Melissa Rakow, Owen Rakow, Leslie Ralston-Rakow, Jessica Rechtschaffer, Jake Roberson, Timothy Roberson, Chris Roosenraad, Bryan Sherwood, Chris Shier, Mark Shier, Andy Socash, Joann Socash, Katherine Spears, Kenneth Stone, Roger Tarr, Ethan Taylor, Peter Taylor, Thomas Taylor, Christopher Thompson, Jeffrey Tyeryar, Jennifer Collier Wilson, Patrick Wilson, and the gentlemen jousters of Denmark

Contents

The Time of the Hundred Years War

Some necessary background to aid in understanding the period

Anno Domini 1381

A year in the life of Sir Geoffrey Peel and the inhabitants of his manor

On Campaign and At War

Life on campaign, deeds of arms, and the trials of battle

Appendix

What We Set Out to Do With This Book

This book is an attempt, from 600 years' distance, to convey a sense of a world undergoing intense change. Society was not the neat hierarchy envisioned by contemporary philosophy or later historians, but untidy and unstable. The shapes of people's lives may seem foreign to us today, but the motives behind them are very familiar: love, fear, faith, ambition.

Our focus is on a single place, time, and group of people: Hampshire, 1381, a knight and his affinity: family and servants, officials and tenants, associates and military company. Through this small community we will try to show you something of life in late fourteenth century England. Our knight's life is different from his grandfather's or grandson's—and different again from the lives of his contemporaries in Scotland, France, or Italy. Rather than try to give you a broad, shallow sketch of "life in the Middle Ages" we hope to use the daily details of our characters' lives to evoke and illustrate their very specific world.

What you'll see herein is the culmination of three years of intense, focused work and many more years of general research, preparation, construction, and acquisition. We have relied on discoveries and interpretations in many historical disciplines, among them archeology, arts, material culture, literature, politics, warfare, and economics. Our photographs feature carefully researched and reconstructed clothing, tools, armor, furnishings, and other items. Many of our artifacts are based closely on surviving items; others are based on manuscript illustrations and paintings. Some are extrapolations, as they must be given the current state of knowledge. We have used backgrounds photographed in England, France, Denmark, and Germany, many of which feature preserved or reconstructed buildings. But in the end, our portrayals of everyday life and work, celebration and tribulation, battle and death can only offer glimpses through a fogged window at people—as real as you or us—who lived in those distant times.

The book is divided into three sections. The first is a brief introduction to the world in which our characters live. In the central part, we take you through a year in the life of our fictional English knight and the people around him. The last part presents a more generalized view of campaign life and war as they might be experienced by our characters. Throughout you will find sidebars highlighting important aspects of medieval English life which affect the lives of our characters.

Our pictures are intended to be candid shots, communicating a moment. We tried to convey the period in our pictures, eliminating the modern and capturing a sense of a specific time and place, as honestly and fully as we are able.

Now look at the picture on this page: it is striking and atmospheric. But while it evokes our characters' era, it does not illustrate its reality. The stone of the cathedral is beautifully carved, but otherwise undecorated. Its niches lack statues of the saints in their painted glory. The roses are lovely and sweet-scented, but they are modern hybrids. Since the picture was taken, we have come to question the gown's decoration. We do believe that a lady might indeed wander a garden within sight of a cathedral, enjoying the scent of blooming roses: the picture evokes the subject matter. But important details are anachronistic: it doesn't illustrate that same subject matter. We have put it here, rather than in the body of the story, in hopes of explaining our aims and method: to depict a specific time and place as fully and accurately as we can.

The sharp-eyed and well-informed will doubtless find what they consider flaws in our pictures or text. Where sources are limited, ambiguous, or contradictory, we have interpreted or extrapolated; in some cases we disagree among ourselves and are continuing our research. We ask you to keep an open mind, and if you have information that we lack, we hope that you will share it with us.

We invite you to look at our pictures, ponder them, and think of people and lives long past. Come with us now. Travel back in time, meet our English knight, and experience a little of his life and world.

THE TIME
OF THE
HUNDRED YEARS
WAR

War, Cruel and Sharp

War defined the medieval world. It was an intrinsic thread woven through feudal society, an inevitable consequence of limited resources and chaotic governmental forms. Nations were ruled by the martial class; warriors were politicians and vice versa. War was often the first resort for settling disputes, from personal insult to property ownership to political allegiance.

The Hundred Years War is the name given to an on-again, off-again conflict between England and France throughout most of the fourteenth century and half of the fifteenth. At its heart lay issues of sovereignty, because the king of England was also the duke of Aquitaine, a French duchy. Centuries of royal marriages had entwined English and French inheritances and loyalties, and centuries of contention had sometimes led to battle.

In 1329, the young King Edward III of England had been on his throne for less than two years. Under the influence of his mother, Isabelle, a princess of France, he swore homage to King Philip VI of France for the duchy of Aquitaine. But contention about French authority over the duchy (and over Edward) began almost immediately. In 1337 Edward renounced his homage. Philip declared the Aquitaine forfeit, and small-scale warfare broke out.

Three years later, Edward went still further and claimed the crown of France, asserting that his claim through his mother (a king's daughter) was better than that of her cousin, Philip (merely a king's grandson). The French denied Edward's belated claim, and the scope of the war broadened from the Aquitaine to the whole of France.

During the course of the war, the fortunes of the two countries rose and fell and rose again. Territory changed hands. Fierce battles were fought. Several times treaties seemed to end the hostilities, but sooner or later the conflict began again. The war ended in 1453 with the battle of Castillon, at which John Talbot, the English commander in France, was killed. Except for the garrison of Calais, English forces withdrew from France.

The time of the Hundred Years War was a time of change in the nature of warfare. As in all wars of any significant duration, military strategies, tactics, and technologies evolved. The nations themselves changed.

To assemble an army for his wars in Scotland, King Edward III in 1327 called forth the English feudal levy, but the resulting army was inadequate. As he set his sights on France, he pursued more reliable ways to raise armies. By the end of the fourteenth century, an English army was composed entirely of paid soldiers. It was not a standing national army, but it was better equipped, better disciplined, and more reliable than a feudal levy.

The French clung for much longer than the English to the idea of the mounted knight's supremacy and to reliance of feudal contingents. But ultimately they followed a similar path, and by the war's end Charles VII created, by ordinance, units of fixed size.

The war also saw gunpowder weapons evolve from novelties to important parts of an army. They were especially useful in the sieges that comprised a large part of the war's military operations, where they could operate from behind prepared wooden and earthen defenses.

At the beginning of the war, knights held pride of place in any army. They were armored much as they had been for hundreds of years, in garments of interlocked iron rings called mail. They wore helmets of iron or steel, and occasionally some additional plates of metal. By the end of the war, full armors of plate were the norm.

Yet at the same time, the mounted knight's primacy on the battlefield was being eclipsed by the power of disciplined infantry. In England this meant dismounted men-at-arms (fully-armored soldiers fighting either from horse or on foot) operating in close cooperation with the famed "yeoman archers," mostly well-to-do commoners armed with the dreaded English war bow—what we now call the longbow.

In the wake of the great fourteenth-century plagues, English commoners took a larger role in society and on the battlefield, and the social and economic distinctions between archers and men-at-arms became less pronounced. By the end of the war, a single family might supply both troop types to a royal army. War had ceased to be the province of aristocrats and their coerced servants. It had become a business.

According to some medieval thinkers, war was the very reason for the existence of the knightly class. Widely held notions of chivalric excellence maintained that war was where a man could best prove his worth. The chivalric class believed that, much as chivalric ideals prescribed rules for knightly conduct, there were rules for the conduct of war and of warriors. One vital point was that a war had to be just; to fight other Christians in an unjust war was a great sin. The burden of justice lay with the king: a loyal subject could follow his ruler to war knowing that his own obedience would absolve him even if the king's justification for war later proved to be false. The guilt would be on the king's head.

It was difficult for the English to take their war to France. The complexity and expense of transporting, supplying, and controlling armies limited their size and the length of time that they could stay in the field. English armies were usually between 4,000 and 6,000 soldiers, though several royal armies exceeded 10,000.

Wars were not just a series of battles. In fact, most of the fighting during the Hundred Years War happened during skirmishes, sieges, and *chevauchées* (de-structive raids). Pitched battles did occur, but they were rare. Both sides understood that, despite knightly eagerness for battle, a pitched battle was always a dangerous endeavor. Once a battle began, too much became uncontrollable, too much rested with chance, and one man—no matter how great his prowess—could do only so much. And even to be on the side of right was no guarantee of success.

When the English did fight a battle, they brought to it a new way of war, developed during their wars against Wales and Scotland. They still divided their army into the traditional three or four groups, but within the groups the armored men-at-arms dismounted and worked in coordination with the archers. Whenever possible, they carefully chose a position to hold, and improved the defensive nature of the terrain. A small body of men-at-arms might be held back for a counterattack or pursuit after the battle. This tactical approach combined solid infantry and massed missile fire. At battles such as Crécy, Poitiers, and Agincourt, it defeated larger French armies that relied primarily on mounted men-at-arms.

Some Battles of the Hundred Years War

1340	Sluys	(English naval victory)
1346	Crécy	(English victory)
1356	Poitiers	(English victory)
1372	La Rochelle	(French naval victory)
1415	Agincourt	(English victory)
1423	Cravant	(English victory)
1424	Verneuil	(English victory)
1429	Patay	(French victory)
1450	Formigny	(French victory)
1453	Castillon	(French victory)

A castle or fortified town offered a place from which a military force could control the land for miles around. The sheltering walls also provided refuge to people and protection for provisions, livestock, and other goods. No army moving through the area could afford to ignore such a presence.

There were both direct and indirect ways to eliminate the threats represented by a fortified place. The most obvious and immediate method was an assault, but walls could be high and well defended, and assaults were costly in lives. Machines could be used to batter at the walls in the hope of making a breach through which soldiers could flood—if the failure of the wall did not itself bring about the garrison's immediate surrender. Specialist engineers could dig mines beneath the walls or towers, then burn the tunnel's supporting timbers, causing the mine and the stonework above it to collapse. Sometimes treachery would bring the defense to an end, as someone inside opened a gate in return for money or some other reward.

The least dramatic, but perhaps most successful, method of forcing capitulation was a siege, in which the fortified place was cut off from supplies until the long-suffering defenders finally surrendered. Yet such a strategy was dangerous to the besiegers as well: disease could ravage the attacking army or, with the countryside's livestock and provisions stockpiled inside the walls, they could themselves run out of food.

When a commander decided to batter at the walls of a fortified place, his siege engineers could call upon a variety of machines. The most formidable of these was the trebuchet. The outer end of its throwing arm was connected to a large sling, in which the missile was placed. A large box slung between A-frame uprights held the counterweight. Anything heavy could be dumped into the box, and a big machine might have a counterweight massing fifteen tons or more. The counterweight was raised by hauling down on the throwing arm; the largest trebuchets used human-operated treadwheels, as shown here. When the counterweight was raised to

its maximum height, the missile was loaded into the sling and the counterweight was released. The box dropped, pulling down the inner end of the throwing arm. The outer end whipped around the pivot, dragging the ropes and sling around in a wide arc. At the crucial moment, the sling sent the missile on its way.

Missiles were commonly stones, sometimes shaped into spheres to give a more reliable trajectory, and could weigh several hundred pounds. But anything that fit into the sling could be thrown, and the heads of executed enemies and even the carcasses of dead animals are recorded as missiles. The latter were intended to promote disease within the fortress's garrison and thereby weaken it.

Other siege machines used other forms of stored energy for power. Catapults relied on the tension in twisted skeins of rope, and springals on the elasticity of their materials. Perriers used the muscle power of a group of men. None could match the trebuchet for range and weight of missile.

Some Sieges of the Hundred Years War

1347 Calais (English win)
1359 Reims (English give up)
1415 Harfleur (English win)
1429 Orleans (English driven off)
1449 Fougères (English win)

Assaults were always a desperate endeavors. The men scaling the walls made a precarious climb, only to be met at the top by determined defenders. It was crucial to make a breach in that defense, to force an opening long enough to get troops onto the wall. The defenders could push a ladder away, dropping the men climbing it to certain injury, if not death. Rocks and stones, stored for the purpose or pried from the battlements, made a lethal rain, and any ordinary weapons could be used to deal death. Assaults worked best when launched by surprise or after the defenders were significantly weakened. Until then, the strong walls gave very effective cover to the defenders.

Crossbows were a favored defensive weapon, since the protection provided by the walls allowed a crossbowman to safely conduct the slow process of spanning (drawing) his bow. His only exposure to the enemy was in the brief moment when he took aim and loosed his bolt.

Sieges could be long and boring, especially to men-at-arms dreaming of great deeds and displays of prowess. Sometimes defenders would issue forth from a gate and defend a barrier fence, to test their mettle against their opponents without completely compromising their defense. Should they be overmatched, they could retreat back within the walls and close the gate before the enemy could follow.

The counterparts to the archers on the walls were the archers of the attacking force. They had no stone walls to protect them, but they could shelter behind earthen banks and wooden pavises (large shields of wooden planks). Arrow ready, an archer could step out for a shot, hoping that no enemy marksman was waiting for him to appear.

Aprincipal strategy for the English throughout the fourteenth century was the *chevauchée*, a cavalry raid on a grand scale. In a *chevauchée*, an army traveled through the countryside bringing devastation. Crops, animals, and property useful to the army were taken, the rest burned or otherwise destroyed. Commoners were terrorized and often killed. In this way the English aimed to demonstrate that the French king could not protect his lands and people. A king so powerless could not be considered a true king, and landholders in the devastated lands would be forced to question their allegiance to him.

A *chevauchée's* fast-moving force was as much by necessity as by design. Supplies were always a problem and foraging was best done in the absence of French defenders. A fortified place might hold rich loot, but if it could not be taken by a quick assault, the army would have to move on, because the English rarely had the necessary siege equipment to deal with fortifications.

Of course there were practical effects of this strategy. The loot gathered by the army would not only supply it as it moved across France, but would also enrich the English Crown, commanders, and individual soldiers. At the same time, the French king and his army were denied those resources.

Although the English preferred to avoid a pitched battle, their planning allowed for that possibility. Indeed, in his campaign of 1359 Edward III designed the devastation in hopes of bringing Philip VI to battle, but Philip refused. Generally, though, the English had little interest in battle. Even the great victories of Poitiers and Agincourt came when the English army was trapped and forced to fight.

From the French perspective, a *chevauchée's* success could be an opportunity. Slowed by the accumulated loot, the marauding Englishmen were easier to catch. Not all French commanders were as shy of battle as Philip.

Yet battle was not the only French response to *chevauchées*. Sometimes they shadowed the English army, threatening battle and either forcing the English away from places that the French wished to protect, or guiding the English advance so as to limit the destruction. In more desperate times, the French themselves devastated the land in front of the English army in an attempt to deprive the English of the supplies and spoils that they sought.

Some Chevauchées (and their commanders)

1342 Brittany (Edward III)

1346 Normandy (Edward III)

1355 Languedoc (Edward, Prince of Wales)

1356 Normandy (John, Duke of Lancaster)

1356 Central France (Edward, Prince of Wales)

1359 Calais to Chartres (Edward III)

1369 Normandy (John, Duke of Lancaster)

1370 Calais to Rennes (Sir John Knollys)

1373 Calais to Gascony (John, Duke of Lancaster)

1380 Calais to Vannes (Thomas, Earl of Buckingham)

1383 Bishop Despenser's "Crusade"

When kings decided to end hostilities, hired soldiers were often simply told that their contract was over and they would no longer be paid. There was rarely an organized system for getting the men home. Soldiers with no better source of income were tempted to turn to banditry and rapine. What else were they to do? War, after all, was a trade they knew. Many found it both more congenial and more lucrative than life at home. Some banded together or simply stayed together in their *routes* (organizational units). These *routiers* (or rutters, as the English called them) then made their own war, much to the detriment of the unfortunates around them.

Often they called themselves "free companies," meaning that they were in business for themselves. Most of the companies retained the structure from their time in the royal armies, not only officers to lead them but also clerks to see that all spoils were accounted for and fairly divided. Sometimes several companies joined to form a larger organization, such as the famed Grand Company, which eventually controlled several castles and even extorted protection money from the pope in Avignon. Smaller and less organized bands of brigands troubled

the countryside as well, robbing and raping as their whim took them.

England had some trouble with returned soldiers who tried to carry on as they had abroad. But the problem was most acute in France, where almost all the fighting of the Hundred Years War took place and where most armies were disbanded.

What the *routiers* did was, of course, against the rules of war and they were officially denounced. The king of France or his deputies sometimes sent armies to destroy them, but the royal forces did not always succeed. Sometimes political machinations were tried to get the *routiers* to go looking for employment somewhere—anywhere—other than France. For example, in 1365 the future constable of France, Bertrand du Guesclin, led free companies into Spain to support France's favored contender for the throne of Castile.

But when hostilities with England flared again, French recruiters were ready, pardons in hand, to hire the companies to fight for France. This was unsurprising and practical, since many of the most renowned and respected generals of the war, for example du Guesclin, rode with or even led some of the free companies.

The men of the companies were Bretons, Spaniards, Germans, Englishmen, and even Frenchmen, but most were Gascons from the southwest corner of France. Whatever their nationalities, the French referred to them as "English." This may have been due in part to the fact that many of the prominent captains among the free companies were Englishmen, finding good business in private war. Notable men such as Sir Hugh Calveley and Sir Robert Knollys made fortunes marauding across France. They saw no contradiction in carrying on the war on their own terms when the king or his deputy had no immediate work for them, then returning to the English king's army whenever the crown renewed martial activity against France.

Some mercenaries, such as Sir John Hawkwood, did not make their names in the French war but traveled to other countries and made their fortunes there. Hawkwood went to Italy with the White Company and became one of the most successful *condottiere* (mercenary) captains in the wars there. Although he never returned to England, he always included a clause in his contracts that he could not be asked to fight against the English king.

Death in battle was the soldier's most immediate risk. Limbs could be hacked off, bodies run through and bones broken. Shock and blood loss killed many who did not die on the spot, and the ever-present threat of infection hung over even the lightly wounded. The wounded, especially though not exclusively those from the other side, were routinely dispatched where they lay, out of mercy or expediency, and then stripped of their armor, weapons, and other valuables. There was no place in an army for a crippled soldier. Should a crippled man make it home, he would find no place for a man who could not work, save perhaps an in alms-house (charitable home for the poor).

The wellborn on the losing side of a battle could hope to be captured, because a wealthy man might pay his captor a substantial ransom in exchange for his freedom—much more than could be made from selling off the equipment of a dead man. But a common soldier was rarely deemed to be worth a ransom.

War devastated the countryside as well, less from the actual destruction of battle than from the scavenging of armies seeking supplies. A friendly army could be just as bad as an invader. Crops and livestock might be destroyed, or buildings burned, to deny them to the enemy. Armies and commanders paid little heed to the concerns of the peasants whose crops, livestock, and buildings were destroyed. Indeed, a peasant attempting to stop such destruction could all too easily become a casualty himself.

And always, women became widows.

A World Changed by the Great Pestilence

The great catastrophe of the fourteenth century was not war, but disease. Called variously "the Great Pestilence," "the Great Death," or simply "the Sickness," the scourge later named the Black Death entered England in 1348 by way of ships arriving from the continent at busy ports, including Bristol and Southampton. It was probably the bubonic plague (*Yersinia pestis*), and it spread from one end of the kingdom to the other, killing over one-third of England's population in less than three years. It was highly capricious, leaving one village virtually untouched while wiping out its neighbor a few miles away. It spread in fits and starts, raging through the warmer seasons and subsiding somewhat during the winter.

The symptoms of the plague were as terrifying as its unpredictability. The variety that afflicted England in 1348-50 appears to have been the bubonic form, in which sufferers developed the characteristic swelling of the lymph nodes known as buboes. Roughly half of those infected by this form of the plague died within a week. Some infections became septicemic, overcoming victims in as little as a day and killing them before buboes could even form. The bubonic and septicemic forms were spread by flea bites and were highly contagious, but the pneumonic form was even more virulent. It was spread via coughing after the plague invaded the victim's lungs, and killed some ninety percent of its victims within three days. All forms of the plague were accompanied by wracking pain, high fever, subcutaneous hemorrhaging (accounting for black spots that spread across the victim's flesh), and foul breath, as well as a host of neurological disorders ranging from twitching to convulsions to delirium. These last lent a particularly terrible aura to the epidemic, as victims raved at people and things only they could see, suggesting strange and malign forces at work.

Variously attributed to God's wrath, malignant astrological confluences, and evil conspiracies, the plague engendered extremes of behavior. Priests led penitential processions through plague-stricken towns, only to be struck down as they walked. On the continent, desperate people joined the flagellant movement, scourging themselves in a vain attempt to cleanse themselves of whatever sins were bringing the plague. It was not a practice that the Church encouraged.

While the plague stalked the land, neighbors shunned one another, crops were not planted, and livestock wandered the fields untended. The very fabric of life seemed about to unravel, and people sought for scapegoats. Any outsider was viewed with suspicion and might be accused of carrying the disease. All over Europe, Jews were accused of spreading the plague by poisoning wells and streams, and entire Jewish communities were massacred. England did not participate in this particular madness, as Jews had been expelled from the kingdom in 1290, but fear and hostility toward Jews lingered for generations.

During the first outbreak, many priests and religious stayed at their posts, ministering to the sick and dying, and often dying themselves as a result; but others fled stricken areas to save their own lives.

At the plague's height, it seemed that the dead far outnumbered the living—and in some places they did. Where possible corpses were interred normally, but eventually in some places they were unceremoniously dumped into mass graves and covered in quicklime. A priest might say a prayer over them—if there was a priest alive to do so. To many, it seemed that the end of the world was at hand.

But the world did go on. By 1351 the Great Death appeared to have passed and, astonishingly, England had not collapsed in chaos. Seeds of change, however, had been planted in many areas.

Reactions to the upheaval and the continued uncertainty were varied and dramatic. Certainly many people—especially while the first outbreak still raged—adopted a sort of "eat, drink, and be merry" attitude, indulging themselves in all the pleasures they could find, in a frenzied attempt to outrun death and despair. Others, seeing the plague as punishment for social corruption and individual sinfulness, turned to prayer, penance, and good works.

The great loss of population meant fewer laborers to produce crops and goods. Landlords found it difficult to get enough laborers to work their fields. Increasingly they had either to permit tenants to rent the land they farmed for cash payments (rather than being bound to the land and customary services), or to hire laborers for inflated wages. This was deeply troubling in the conservative English society, and during the last half of the fourteenth century the parliament passed several statutes trying to lower wage payments to pre-plague levels. Predictably, the measures failed.

Standards of living rose for artisans and laborers, but landowners' incomes were increasingly strained. They sought new ways of securing their finances and living standards, such as converting idle arable land (land suitable for farming) to pasture or more closely enforcing manorial fees and fines. The Crown too sought new ways to raise revenues. Poll (per-head) taxes in 1377, 1379, and 1380 met increasing protest and evasions—one-third of the population simply vanished from the tax rolls between 1377 and 1380.

Constant awareness of death became a part of life. Morbid images of death haunted paintings and manuscripts. In churches, the wealthy began to decorate their monuments with *memento mori*, bizarre and graphic reminders of inevitable death and decay.

Then, only eleven years after the plague had passed, England learned that it was not gone. A relatively mild recurrence in 1361 was followed by outbreaks in 1374 and 1379. The visitation in 1374 became known as the children's plague because of the high mortality among those born since the earlier outbreaks and lacking acquired immunity. The recurrence in 1379 seems to have had relatively low human mortality, but was deadly among sheep and cattle. Although none of these outbreaks compared to the first in terms of mortality and sheer horror, plague would recur periodically for several centuries, and fear of its unpredictable return became a permanent part of the English mentality.

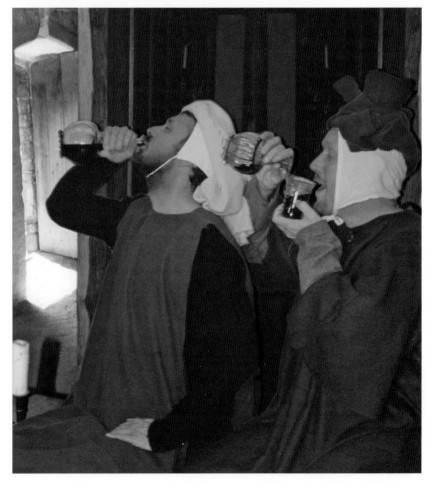

The Church in a Time of Change and Distress

In fourteenth-century England, as in the rest of western Europe, to be Christian was to be Roman Catholic. By 1381, England had been thoroughly Christian for centuries—any pre-Christian practices that survived had lost their religious content and were simply custom, or at best superstition. In fact, England was one of the most orthodox countries in Europe; there was no Inquisition in England.

The Church was enormously important in every person's life, and most people encountered the Church one way or another virtually every day. As many as one adult in fifty took priestly or other religious vows. Although during the fourteenth century universities were attracting more and more lay students, they were still dominated by clerics as faculty, staff, and students. A small abbey or monastery might house only a handful of people, but a large one was the center of a substantial estate. Monks, lay brothers (members of a religious community who were responsible for manual or administrative rather than spiritual labor), tenants, and servants performed all the work necessary to keep the establishment operating. About one-fourth of English agricultural land was held by the Church, and many people were tenants on Church lands.

There were some five hundred religious houses in England, and in towns and cities there were numerous parish churches and religious houses, ranging from tiny hole-in-the-wall churches that served single neighborhoods to huge cathedrals and monasteries. In the 1380s, the town of Southampton, with a population of about 4,000, supported five parishes, a charity hospital, and a Franciscan friary within its walls, and nearby an Augustinian house and a leper hospital with a chapel.

For virtually everyone in England, Christianity was a matter of fact, not of faith. Although theology was constantly a matter of debate, the goal was to clarify and perfect Christian doctrine, not to challenge or reject it. The Christian worldview was the only one on offer, and it pervaded all aspects of life from judging the justness of a war to marking the hours by church bells, and from required attendance at Sunday Mass to the desperate fear of dying unshriven (without confessing and being absolved of sin) and therefore being eternally damned to the torments of Hell. Biblical and liturgical language and imagery were everywhere and shaped every English person's patterns of thought.

In towns and cities, laypeople formed fraternities or guilds, organizing for social service and mutual support. Fraternities (joined by both men and women, despite the name) were fundamentally religious associations: they usually were dedicated to a patron saint, and operated under the auspices of a parish or other church. But they tended to develop economic purposes as well; many became linked to specific trades or crafts, and in some towns and cities guild membership was a de facto requirement for civic office.

But despite the Church's ideal of unity and uniformity among all believers, dissension and division were inevitable. Deep theological study led some scholars to question Church teachings or practices. Some of those questions led to doctrinal change or institutional reforms, but others were condemned as heresy. The Church vigorously condemned heresy and heretics as a disease on the body of the Church—a heretic could contaminate those who listened to him and lead them to damnation. Although England was relatively free of heresy during most of the Middle Ages, the English Church guarded against it vigilantly.

But the great scandal of the Church at this time was

not heresy; it was the Great Schism, caused by the existence of two competing popes. A papal election was called in 1378, only a year after the Papacy's return to Rome following nearly seventy years in the French city of Avignon—and fifty years of French popes. With a number of cardinals absent, and under pressure from the Roman citizens to elect a Roman, the College of Cardinals hastily elected an Italian, Bartolomeo Prignano, who took the name Urban VI and ruled from Rome. Friction arose almost immediately between Pope Urban and the cardinals, and many of those who had been present at the election repudiated him. Within months, a second conclave elected Robert of Geneva, who took the name Clement VII and resided in Avignon. The Schism was to last for nearly forty years, exacerbated by international politics: Urban was supported by England and most of the Empire, while Clement was supported by France, Castile, and Scotland.

Throughout Europe there flourished numerous religious orders of monks (members of a cloistered community or an order of hermits), canons (priests living communally under a rule called a canon), friars (itinerant preachers who lived by begging), and nuns (members of a religious order of women). In England, the most populous orders were Benedictine monks and Augustinian canons. Only about one-third of religious men and women in England belonged to orders; the majority were secular priests. There were about ten times as many men as women in religious life.

Just as lay society was divided into many levels and groups—peasant, artisan, merchant, soldier, gentry, nobility, and royalty—so the Church had its hierarchy. It was ruled by the pope, or supreme pontiff, elected by a small group of senior clerics, the cardinals. Most of the cardinals, in turn, were bishops (heads of dioceses). A diocese was generally a city and its surrounding area; in England in 1381 there were seventeen dioceses, and the bishop of each had his seat at the cathedral in the main city of his diocese. For most laypeople, daily contact with the Church was through the local parish and the priest or priests associated with it. Diocesan or "secular" clergy were ordained by their local bishop and subject to him, rather than the rules of a religious order.

In England, as elsewhere in Europe, the Church played an active role in community and nation—not just in faith and religious practice, but in functions that would later come to be considered lay responsibilities, such as large-scale agriculture, education, health care, and even government. Many bishops held important offices in the royal administration: by 1381 William of Wykeham, the Bishop of Winchester, had also served the king as keeper of the privy seal and as chancellor.

The Church functioned not only as a major landowner but also as a provider of many important social services. The universities still operated under Church auspices; both cathedrals and religious orders operated schools; priests, monks, and nuns provided elementary education to children in towns and wealthy households. Many orders ran hospitals and schools, cared for orphans, and fed the poor.

Meanwhile the religious orders in England, as in the rest of Christendom, continually struggled between asceticism and pragmatism, mysticism and service, withdrawal from the world and engagement with it. Each order achieved its unique balance and endeavored to hold to it against competing pressures. Many orders went through cycles of decadence—relaxation of rules, preoccupation with worldly issues—and reform. By the end of the fourteenth century, a number orders were in a relatively decadent phase, visible even to the laity.

To some degree orders, and individual clerics, had become victims of their own success. Lay patrons, seeking salvation for themselves and their families, had donated money and property to church institutions over generations, until many religious houses and cathedrals had become conspicuously wealthy.

Now, although manual labor, prayer, and spiritual study were still nominally the core of cloistered life, many religious had drifted from their traditions of self-supporting labor toward the business of administering their lands and their commerce. New orders, such as the Cistercians, were founded in attempts at reform. At the end of the eleventh century the Cistercians branched off from the Benedictine order, which had become established and wealthy, and in many monastaries had strayed from the rigor of its original rule. Rather than delegating manual labor to lay brothers or tenants, Cistercians performed their own: working the fields, tending the flocks, even splitting wood with ax and mallet to supply the monastary with fuel. But over time the Cistercians, too, struggled to maintain the austerity of their discipline in the face of growing wealth and power; and like other orders before them they went through a series of revivals and reforms.

Secular clerics needed to support themselves, and pursued income through appointment to a benefice (salaried church office) such as a chantry (privately funded liturgy, usually a series of Masses for the dead) or employment as a chaplain to a fraternity or a wealthy household. Numerous priests held more than one benefice and hired other priests to perform some of their duties. Bishops took advantage of the wealth of their dioceses, and often their own multiple benefices; many of them were as powerful, and lived as lavishly, as any lay noble. Some abbots (superiors of monasteries), in their turn, were nearly as powerful and extravagant as the bishops. Women's houses were criticized for permitting their nuns to neglect their liturgical offices, indulge in rich dress and diet, read romances, and keep pets.

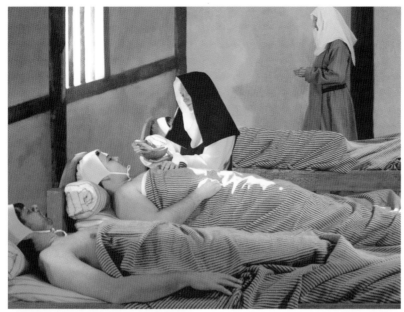

The worldliness and corruption of many clergy contrasted powerfully with both the Church's ideals and the example of those who still lived by them. Stories of misbehaving religious men and women were widespread and sometimes lurid—priests who wore lay clothes and cut their tonsures (the partly shaven heads that designated professed clergy) as small as possible; young monks who carried swords and brawled with apprentices in the streets; nuns who entertained men within their cloisters; priests who gave the sacraments while being thoroughly corrupt and sinful themselves. Following as they did the poor performance of many clergy during the plague, these abuses contributed to a growing anticlerical sentiment throughout the country.

But neither the uncorrupted clergy nor the laity were passive in the face of these evils. Preachers and writers were vociferous in criticism of abuses. Both clerical and lay critics objected to the degree of royal control over election of bishops; the outrageous lifestyles of clergy; religious landlords' demands on their tenants; and the greed of Church officials such as pardoners, who extorted money from the laity in exchange for pardons from sin. In the 1370s an Oxford theologian, John Wycliffe, publicly criticized the Church for its wealth and many abuses, and advocated subjecting the Church to civil authority. Initially he gained wide support, some of it from influential churchmen and noblemen. But he moved from institutional reform to theological disputes, and in 1382 he was condemned at a synod in London and his writings were banned.

The widespread anticlerical sentiment was directed at individuals, and at the Church as an institution, but not at the Christian faith. It developed in parallel with a deep and growing devotion to individual piety and practices, spurred at least in part by the experience of the plague and the resulting upsurge in concern about the afterlife. The cycle of prayers to the Blessed Virgin (Mary, the mother of Jesus) that would one day become the Rosary was popularized during the fourteenth century. Books of Hours enabled the literate and wealthy faithful to perform abbreviated versions of the Divine Office (daily prayers and readings performed by religious communities) in their homes. Devotion to *Corpus Christi* (the body of Christ) grew and became popular as a civic observance. Writers and spiritual guides developed devotional regimens suited to those who lived "in the world." A devout laywoman (or man) might seek to spend her last years in a religious house, or at least to be buried in the habit of her favored order.

England and France

In England, by 1381 Richard II was in the fourth year of his reign. He was fourteen years old, and though by custom a man, he was still legally a minor and could not rule on his own. In 1380, after three years of growing dissatisfaction with the council appointed to rule during Richard's minority, the parliament had dismissed the nine council members, but without appointing replacements. As 1381 opened the government was still in flux but dominated by officers of the royal household and led by the chancellor, Simon Sudbury, archbishop of Canterbury.

Negotiations for Richard's marriage were underway, as the realm would be more secure once he had sired an heir. The choice of bride was critical: it was expected to establish alliances that would last for decades—and foreclose others.

In France, Charles VI had been king for less than a year. He was only twelve, and officially considered still a boy. His father's brothers, the dukes of Anjou, Berry, and Burgundy, and his mother's brother, the duke of Bourbon, nominally shared the rule of France. But his paternal uncles were united only in their eagerness to remove the most competent and loyal of the late king's councilors; each pursued his own advantage.

Taxes, imposed "for the war" and spent without driving out the English, aroused deep resentment among the French people. On his deathbed the late king had renounced the hearth (per-household) tax, and the government's subsequent efforts to impose new taxes led to riots.

The war between England and France went through times of intense military activity, periods of low-level skirmishing, campaigns involving foreign but partisan countries, and even stretches of peace. During the late 1370s the English suffered reverses in France, and in 1381 English enthusiasm for the war was low although tensions remained high. In the previous year, the earl of Buckingham had led a *chevauchée* from Calais to Brittany, and as 1381 began he still had an army there, ready to support the English candidate in the contest for the duchy of Brittany.

Meanwhile, King Richard's unpopular but experienced uncle John, duke of Lancaster, sought to open a second front against France by way of Spain.

Richard maintained his grandfather Edward's claim to the throne of France. Like his grandfather, he used the heraldry shown above, which quarters the arms of England ("Gules, three leopards Or") with those of France ("Azure, semé of fleurs de lys Or") to represent his assertion of sovereignty over both kingdoms.

At the beginning in 1337

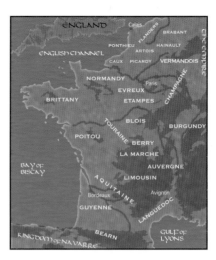

At the end in 1453

During the course of the war, control of French territory flowed back and forth between France and England. The high points of English success were around 1360, when Edward III was aggressively and skillfully pursuing his claim, and in the 1420s, after Henry V's great successes. But during the 1370s the English lost many of their earlier gains, due in large part to the successful strategies of Charles V and his redoubtable constable, Bertrand du Guesclin.

Throughout the fourteenth century the Aquitaine was still the heart of English territory in France, but the border moved back and forth across the northern and eastern boundaries, where local lords turned "English" or "French" following shifting advantage and their own interests.

Highwater marks in English dominion

1360

1429

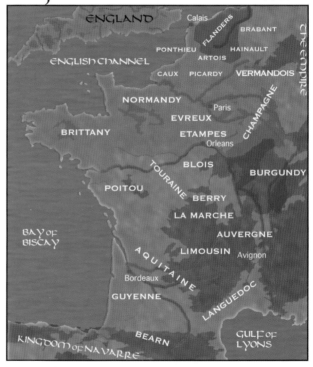

In 1360 the Treaty of Bretigny, which followed the capture of Charles V at the battle of Poitiers, expanded England's control to the widest area it would reach during the fourteenth century. The treaty returned control of the Aquitaine and ceded additional lands. For his part, Edward III gave up his claim to the French crown. But after Charles returned from captivity he encouraged his nobles to purse low-level hostilities, and eventually du Guesclin regained much of what had been negotiated away.

After Henry V's death in 1422 his infant son, Henry, was crowned king of both England and France under the terms of the Treaty of Troyes, negotiated after the battle of Agincourt and the subsequent Normandy campaign. French resistance to Henry VI centered on Charles, the son of Charles VI who had been disinherited by the treaty. The duke of Burgundy, believing that Charles had conspired to murder his father, allied himself with the English, and Anglo-Burgundian forces pushed English territories to the greatest extent achieved during the Hundred Years War. But Joan of Arc's victories on behalf of Charles, beginning at Orléans in 1429, would start to undo English successes yet again.

England and Hampshire

The county of Hampshire, on the south coast of England, is the setting for the heart of our story. Southampton, on a peninsula between the Rivers Test and Itchen, is one of England's leading ports, a key entry point for trade (in particular with Bordeaux and Genoa), and often the embarkation point for armies headed to France. Winchester, to the north, was the capital of the ancient Saxon kingdom of Wessex, and in 1381 is still an important city and the seat of Bishop William of Wykeham. In the southwest, the New Forest is a favored royal hunting preserve. The coastal areas are mostly forest and march, poor for agriculture. The chalk downs (uplands) to the north are good for grazing sheep. The river valleys are the most fertile areas, suitable for grain and other agricultural crops.

The Peel family has been established in Hampshire since time out of mind, and Sir Geoffrey holds two other manors in Hampshire and several in other counties. Sir Geoffrey is one of few lay landlords in the Dunbury area; most of the land in this part of Hampshire is held by the Church, in particular by the abbey of St. Mary's in Winchester. Sir Geoffrey himself is not a gregarious man, and of all his manors his favorite is the secluded Dunbury. It lies near the Test about twenty-five miles north of Southampton, near the town of Stockbridge and the villages of Over, Middle, and Nether Wallop. There we will follow him, his family and servants, tenants and soldiers, through the year of grace 1381.

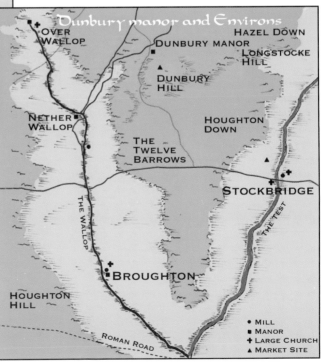

Anno Domini
1381

SPRING

Twelfth Night is the Feast of the Epiphany, marking the visit of the Three Kings to the infant Jesus. This is the last day of the Christmas celebrations and the cusp of a new year. By the agricultural reckoning, it marks the beginning of Spring.

Every day starts early for a cook, but for Philip Doughty, cook of the Peel household, this is an especially early day. Sir Geoffrey celebrates Twelfth Night with guests, entertainment, and an elaborate feast.

Philip arrives in the kitchen before dawn to find the kitchen workers rebuilding the fires in the hearth from embers hoarded overnight under a pottery curfew (from the French *couvre-feu*, fire-cover).

He planned the menu for the night's feast long ago, and now he sets his staff to work. The youngest members of the kitchen staff draw water and chop firewood; Philip must have an ample supply of suitably sized wood so that he can adjust the fires as needed throughout the day. The rest of the staff starts to gather the foodstuffs that Philip needs from the various places that supply the kitchen: breads and pastries from the pantry; wine and ale from the buttery; birds, eggs, and dairy products from the poultry; other food stores from the larder; and dishes from the scullery.

Philip, like the master who taught him, has memorized all his best recipes and runs his kitchen rigorously, keeping everyone on the staff busy with preparations: chopping, grinding, mixing, and seasoning to his exacting specifications. Some tasks, such as preparing the mixtures of seasonings and spices, he reserves to himself, not trusting anyone else to do them just right.

Philip begins preparing the meat courses by mixing spices for an egredouce (sweet and sour) sauce to accompany a dish of coneys (rabbits), then turns to chopping the coney carcasses into serving pieces.

A manor's food came from a variety of sources, both local and foreign. Most meat, poultry, game, and fish came either from the manor itself or from nearby markets. Many crops were grown on either the lord's lands or those of his tenants. Other foods, from elsewhere in England or from the continent, could be bought from traders or retailers. Exotic goods, such as cinnamon, pistachios, and dates, were imported from as far away as Asia via the Mediterranean, traveling north to England through networks of fairs on the continent or arriving by ships, such as the Genoese galleys that called annually at Southampton.

Preparations for the big feast keep the kitchen busy all day, right up to the meal and even during it, as the food must be at the moment of perfection when it arrives on Sir Geoffrey's table. Hot foods must be served hot and cold foods served cold, to keep the diners' humors (essential body fluids kept in correct proportions by proper diet) in balance.

Today Edward Manser, Sir Geoffrey's body servant, has extra duties attending the table and Sir Geoffrey's guests. He carries dishes of sweetmeats for the guests to nibble before the meal.

All the bustle means that young Henry Doughty manages to avoid more of his chores than usual. It will not be long, however, before Ursula spots him idling on the windowsill and sends him off to the pantry to fetch some breadcrumbs to thicken a sauce.

Dionisia Lene, one of the household women, takes down a pitcher from the crockery stored atop the aumbry (cupboard), for mixing spiced wine to be served at the end of the meal.

As master of the kitchen, Philip Doughty commands a complex undertaking. He depends on his wife, Ursula, to act as his lieutenant throughout the demanding process of cooking the many dishes and arranging them for service.

Some dishes need last-minute touches before leaving the kitchen. While Ursula shucks mussels to be simmered in broth, Beatrice Michel garnishes the roasted capons with powder forte (a sharp spice mixture) before they are served forth. Henry looks on, eager for the leftovers that will soon be coming back to the kitchen.

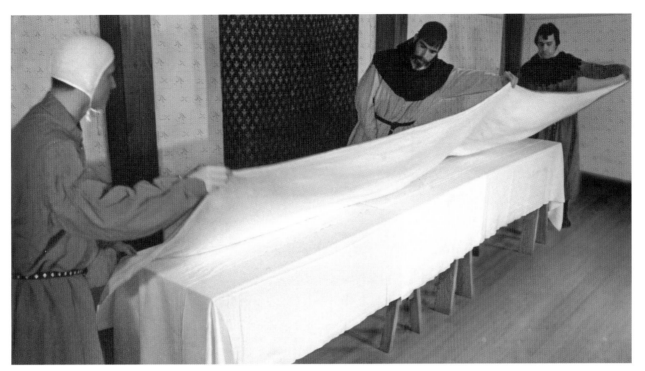

Edward Manser and Simon Crispin, one of the household varlets (mid-level servants), set up the high table under the supervision of Stephen Wallis, the gentleman of the hall. The cloth is laid with care, because a well-run household must show linens that are spotlessly white, smoothed to perfection, and correctly arrayed.

Once the table linens are laid, the places may be set. Stephen lays Sir Geoffrey's finest knife at the knight's seat. The knife is part of a matched set that includes a pair of large carving knives that will be used later in the meal.

The pewter trencher plates and salt are not as fine as the silver tableware becoming more common in knightly households, but Sir Geoffrey has spent money on fine imported glassware and has ordered it set out for the feast to impress his guests.

Stephen draws wine from a cask in the buttery. This is a task he will perform throughout the meal, carrying the wine to the hall in a finely made pewter flagon. The flagon and other serving dishes will rest on the dresser or sideboard when not being carried to table.

When no one is looking, one of the kitchen grooms (lower-level servants) filches a morsel of the coney before it is carried to the lord's table.

The guests begin to arrive. Dunbury's isolated location means that not all who might have come will brave the cold weather and difficult road conditions. Some of Sir Geoffrey's other manors would have been more convenient for the guests, but Sir Geoffrey prefers to entertain them here in his favorite house.

The style of the house, with its upper-level hall, goes back centuries; ground-level halls are more popular in these modern times, but its traditional structure is one of the reasons that Sir Geoffrey favors Dunbury.

Stephen Wallis stands upon the stairs leading to the great hall. He greets the guests as they arrive, inviting them to come in from the cold courtyard to the hall where the tables have been prepared and hot drinks await.

Chief among the guests is William Cressy, an old friend of the family. His father was a brother-in-arms to Sir Geoffrey's late father when they both fought in France under Edward of Woodstock, the late prince of Wales and father of the present king. William keeps up a military connection with the Peels and serves as a man-at-arms when Sir Geoffrey goes to war. In peaceful times, such as this year, he is a frequent and welcome visitor, with his store of gossip and chivalrous stories.

Master Gerrit le Flemyng is another guest: one of the numerous Flemish wool merchants living in Southampton, who handles many of Sir Geoffrey's business affairs. He and his wife, Maria, have traveled with their servants up the River Test by boat, a less taxing trip than riding the frozen roads. Once inside, Master le Flemyng asks for a private talk with Sir Geoffrey, to deliver a letter that he has brought. It arrived in England by ship, carried by a traveler who had business with le Flemyng and knew that the merchant had connections with Sir Geoffrey.

Sir Geoffrey receives le Flemyng in his parlor, away from the bustle of the hall. He is wearing a warm fur hat, more a necessity than a luxury for him in the cold weather since he lost his hair to a fever. Even indoors, the drafts can be chilly.

The men read the letter at the parlor window, where the January sunlight streams through the waxed linen. The message is from Sir Geoffrey's old comrade Sir John Stratton. Sir John lives in Gascony, the southern region of the Aquitaine and one of the key English holdings in France. He expects to be named constable of Bordeaux and is beginning to think about strengthening the defense of the region. Stratton wants Sir Geoffrey to accept an indenture (contract) to serve as the commander of a garrison north of Bordeaux. He can offer no special bonuses other than the right of *patis* (permission to use the income of the region to pay expenses) and asks that Sir Geoffrey take on this service more out of friendship than for practical reward.

It is a request that Sir Geoffrey must consider carefully.

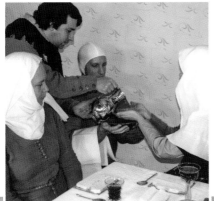

The meal begins with a handwashing ceremony. Simon gently pours scented water from the ewer over a guest's hands. The water flows into the bowl held by Edward, who has a clean linen towel draped over his arm for the guest to wipe her hands dry.

Sir Geoffrey sits in the center of the table beneath his cloth of estate, made of rich fabric given to him many years ago by the late Prince of Wales. At his right hand sits his wife, Lady Joan. To his left is his mother Emmota, the dowager Lady Peel, visiting for the Christmas season from her dower manor south of Andover. Sir Geoffrey's table is also graced today by John Everard and his wife, Agnes. John is the steward of Sir Geoffrey's manor at Somborne, a larger and more prosperous property than Dunbury, though not as near to Sir Geoffrey's heart. At the end of the table sits Dame Katherine de Anne, Lady Joan's widowed cousin, who lives at Dunbury while considering her prospects for a new marriage.

James Warde, the bailiff (administrative officer) at Dunbury, ceremonially carves the meat before Sir Geoffrey. James is one of Dunbury's more well-off tenants, and an ambitious man; he has studied the intricate skills required to serve a lord's table, and he does well by Sir Geoffrey. Once he has served Sir Geoffrey and Lady Joan, the roast will be removed to the dresser for less formal—but faster—carving so that it can be brought back to the table and served out. The diners will share the meal two to a plate, or "mess."

To Lady Peel's left sits William Cressy, who amuses her with stories and gossip. Beyond him are the le Flemyngs, honored to be seated with the gentry.

While a great lord can afford to employ a servant solely to make music, Sir Geoffrey is not so rich. Among the household women is Julian Wallis, the widow of Stephen's late brother, a Southampton wayte (member of the municipal watch, who were secondarily musicians), who taught her to sing, juggle, and play several instruments. Most days she attends on Lady Joan, but tonight her only duty is to provide music for the feast. She plays her harp and sings while Sir Geoffrey's godson Edward Upham demonstrates his courtly skills by accompanying her on a vielle. Lady Peel and William listen with educated appreciation, but Master le Flemyng, well fed and tired from his journey, drifts off, leaving his poor wife stranded at the end of the table, valiantly trying to appear pleased.

A new day begins at Dunbury. Sir Geoffrey's man Edward Manser, and Lady Joan's woman Marjorie atte Well, have been awake for some time. Before the Peels arise, their servants must dress, put away the pallets on which they slept, and lay out clothing appropriate to the day for their master and mistress. Edward has taken down the wooden shutters over the window, making the room bright but cold. Now the Peels are awake and Marjorie opens the bed's curtains for the day. She will knot the bottom of each panel and tuck the knot within the body of the curtain to make a bulbous, decorative arrangement. Lady Joan huddles in a cloak as she loosens her hair from the night's braid.

Sir Geoffrey still wears his sleeping coif (head covering), though he has already donned his shirt and braes (drawers) of fine white linen. Edward helps him to put on a pair of hosen. Each will cover the knight's foot and leg with warm, elastic wool.

Once dressed, the Peels will hear Mass in their chapel, then break their fast with bread, cheese, and wine or ale.

John Arundel is one of Sir Geoffrey's tenants. Here he and his family break the night's fast. Breakfast is traditionally neither large nor important—just a light meal, eaten early and quickly, to fuel the morning's labor until the main meal at midday. Laborers and craftsman eat a breakfast of pottage, a mush of bread and grains soaked in ale. The very young and the elderly would get the same meal soaked in milk.

John's wife, Avis, distributes the morning pottage to John and their three surviving children. Their daughter Elizabeth (nicknamed Elisota) is the oldest. There is a gap of some years between her and Tomkyn. And finally there is young John, the third of the couple's children to bear that name. Neither of the previous two survived his second year. Once the meal is finished the family will disperse to their tasks: John to the fields, Avis and Elisota to work around the house and toft (yard, garden, and outbuildings), and the boys to errands, light chores, and later to playing with friends.

The Arundels' house, although strongly made, is far less fine than the manor house. The floor of the main room is of packed earth, and the fireplace is an old-fashioned hearth in the center of the floor, vented through gaps in the roof. The interior partition wall is bare wattle (woven sticks). John rebuilt it just before Christmas, and he will cover it over with daub (a mix of clay, straw, dung, and hair) as soon as he finds the time. Avis is starting to lose patience.

Father Alan celebrates daily Mass in the Peels' chapel. This is an unusually elaborate chapel for a private home, and Father Alan wears unusually fine vestments for a private chaplain. Few households have a chapel in the house; usually families like the Peels serve as patrons of the parish church in the manor village or the nearest town. Such patronage may take the form of donating a chapel, furnishing vestments or altar plate, or endowing a stipend for a priest. In many cases family members are buried in a prominent location within the church, under an engraved brass plaque or a sculpted effigy.

But Dunbury village's church, like half the village, belongs to a manor owned by the abbey of St. Mary in Winchester. The nuns operate the church as a subsidiary chapelry of the abbey: they send hired priests to serve it and claim all its tithes and offerings for the abbey. Often the priests have held several benefices and rarely visited Dunbury. Since before Sir Geoffrey's grandfather's day, the village (with the Peels' support) has tried to have the church converted to a parish, subject to the Winchester diocese and served by a resident priest; but the nuns have held on adamantly. Thus deprived of an opportunity for patronage, the Peels and their several generations of wealthy, pious wives have focused their devotion and money on the family chapel.

At present the Peel household supports two Augustinian canons: Father Alan, the chaplain and tutor, and Father Paul, Sir Geoffrey's secretary and Lady Joan's confessor.

Lady Joan attends Mass daily, and Sir Geoffrey most days; they expect that the family and servants will do the same. So attendance at daily Mass is usual, but for many among the household it consists of little more than being passively present. The liturgy is performed entirely in Latin and, while many people know a few Latin catchphrases and maybe a prayer or two, few can follow the Mass in its entirety. For their part, many priests are accused of gabbling or mumbling through the rite so quickly and indistinctly that nobody could understand them even in English. Father Alan is well trained and speaks clearly, but he stands at the front of the chapel, with his back to the congregation virtually the entire time. At least the Peel chapel is too small for a screen between the congregation and the altar, which would separate them yet further from the rite.

Preaching is one of the most important aspects of pastoral work, and Father Alan takes it very seriously. Like the more educated members of the clergy, he has been formally trained to preach in both English and Latin to a variety of audiences: urban and rural, lay and clerical, private and public. Parish priests have access to handbooks laying out annual programs of preaching, and preaching orders such as Franciscans and Dominicans design their churches to maximize preaching space. Father Alan, conscious of how little his flock comprehends of the liturgy, makes the most of his opportunity to expound on it informally, in English.

Another morning, and Marjorie atte Well dresses Lady Joan's hair for the day. On most days this is a quick process, as Lady Joan wears the practical linen wimple and veil. But today visitors are expected, so Marjorie creates a more formal arrangement. She parts the hair in the middle and gathers each side near the temple, where she braids it and ties it with a cord. The end of each braid is tucked under and secured with a hair pin, and a light silken veil is pinned to fall behind the braids. On ceremonial occasions Lady Joan adds a frontlet (decorative band), sewn with river pearls, at her hairline.

Lady Joan and Marjorie are wearing essentially the same garments: a woolen gown over a long-sleeved kirtle, a white linen smock, knee-high woolen hosen, and lightweight leather shoes. The differences between them are in quality. Lady Joan's red kirtle (underdress) is made of Italian silk, dyed "in grain," that is, with imported kermes (Mediterranean insects which yield a rich red dye). It laces tightly to achieve a fashionable silhouette, and its closely-fitted sleeves fasten with tiny golden buttons. Marjorie's red kirtle (below) is made of linen dyed with local madder root; it is loose enough to pull on over her head and the sleeves are not fitted or buttoned. Lady Joan's green gown (overdress) is generously lined and trimmed with expensive budge (lambskin); Marjorie's brown gown (dyed with walnut—inexpensive but corrosive, over time, to the wool) is lined in the bodice with cat's fur, but elsewhere with linen. Lady Joan's girdle (belt) is woven of white silk and decorated with silver studs; Marjorie's is of leather decorated with pewter. Marjorie's most luxurious accessory is her purse, made from a gift of scraps from Lady Joan's kirtle.

Marjorie's headdress is practical for everyday; first she drapes a white linen

wimple under her chin and around her neck, and pins it at the crown of her head. Then she lays a long rectangle of linen on top of her head and twists the ends into ropes which she wraps around her head, tucking the ends under securely.

Linen is the best material for clothes that must be cleaned often: shirts, smocks, braes, aprons. It washes well and can be bleached to dazzling whiteness with well-aged urine. Wool is preferred for most other garments. Depending on how it is spun, woven, and processed, it can be thick and water-resistant for caps and cloaks; elastic for use in hosen; luxurious for gentry clothing; or sturdy for laborers. It does not wash well, so woolen clothes are sponged and brushed frequently; periodically they are cleaned by rubbing in an absorbent material

such as clay to pull out dirt and oils, and brushing it out. Worn next to the skin, the often-washed linen protects the woolen stuff from sweat and oils, and extends the time between cleanings.

Women's hosen come only to the knee and are held in place with garters. Lady Joan's garters are narrow bands of heavy silk, with buckles and ends of silver. The buckles were cast in molds made from cuttlebone; the internal shell of a cuttlefish is firm, fine-grained, and easy to carve, making it ideal for casting small items of precious metal. Her shoes are of red leather, tooled in a floral pattern.

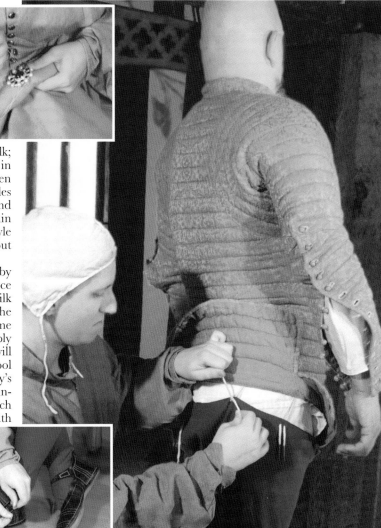

Sir Geoffrey finishes dressing for the day. Over his shirt, Edward Manser has buttoned him into a doublet, a short, quilted garment which fits tightly over the arms and below the waist but is cut full in the chest, to give the desirable silhouette: deep-chested and slim-hipped. The doublet is made from three layers of linen covered with an outer layer of brocaded silk; two thin layers of cotton wool (unspun cotton) in the chest area provide a little extra firmness when all the layers are quilted together. The armholes are cut so deep that Sir Geoffrey's shoulders, and the muscles of his chest and back, are within the sleeves; this *grande assiette* (big armhole) style permits a wide range of arm movement without pulling up the body and skirt.

Sir Geoffrey's hosen are being trussed up by points (lacings) to the skirt of the doublet. Once the hosen are attached, Edward will buckle silk garters below Sir Geoffrey's knees to keep the hosen smooth over the calf while relieving some of the stress at the knee so that he can comfortably bend his legs. Over the doublet Sir Geoffrey will wear the outermost layer, a gown of fine wool lavishly lined with coney. It is one of Sir Geoffrey's everyday gowns, cut just below the knee and undecorated, unlike his Twelfth Night gown, which is made of samite (heavy silk twill), lined with "pured" miniver (white belly fur of Russian squirrels), and elaborately dagged (scalloped) at the sleeve edges.

Edward finishes tying the latchets of Sir Geoffrey's shoes. Their dyed surfaces have been scraped and tooled in a decorative pattern.

John Arundel and Thomas Stockbridge dress for their day's work. Like Sir Geoffrey they wear linen shirt and braes, and wool hosen. But their hosen are old-fashioned: the upper edge comes to a single point in front and falls below the buttocks in back, while Sir Geoffrey's comes to the hipbone all around. Thus the tenants' hosen need only a single attachment point: John pins his hosen to his braes with annular (ring-shaped) brooches, and Thomas ties his to a leather braegirdle (belt over his braes). This leaves their braes mostly uncovered, but since they never wear a doublet alone—a fashionable look indulged in mostly by the upper ranks—they have no concern about their braes showing. Instead they wear old-fashioned tunics, knee-length and long-sleeved, of frieze (heavy, coarse wool). In the cold January weather they need more warmth, but a cloak would be awkward when working. So they will layer on a second woolen tunic, and a second pair of hosen.

Like many of Sir Geoffrey's tenants, Thomas favors a linen coif—it may be old-fashioned, but it gives a little extra warmth on this cold morning.

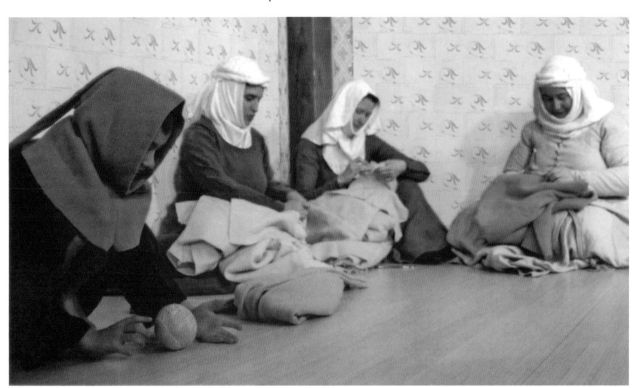

While Henry Doughty plays with a leather ball, Julian Wallis joins Ursula Doughty and Beatrice Michel to make new clothes from their Twelfth Night cloth allotments, part of their annual wage. Like most knightly families, the Peels contract servants on an annual basis, and the wage comprises board, a small cash payment, and a semi-annual gift of cloth sufficient to make one set of garments.

Raw materials were generally more valuable than the time spent to make them into things. Nothing was thrown away that could be repaired. Items that were no longer suitable but still serviceable could be sold to the less fortunate. The rich, as ever, were less bound by such considerations, but even they were frugal with what they considered valuable.

One result of this was a thriving trade in used items. Certain tradesmen even specialized in such goods.

Upholders bought and sold used clothing, garments which financial fortune or misfortune, change in physical or social stature, or the owner's death had rendered available for sale. Their stock was unpredictable, because they depended on individual sellers' whims, and would-be buyers could not count on finding anything usable. But in an era when every garment was made by hand, discovering a well-fitting garment—perhaps of a cut, fabric, or color otherwise unaffordable—was worth the search.

Cobblers did not make shoes, but repaired shoes that were no longer wearable. When a shoe was past repairing, the cobbler salvaged parts, for instance by cutting the upper part of a shoe into pieces to use whatever leather was still good, or cutting off the usable bits of a worn sole before sewing on the replacement leather. Sometimes shoemakers deliberately destroyed used shoes so that they could not be repaired by a cobbler, thus eliminating a source of competition for their new shoes.

Textiles were both vital to daily life and labor-intensive to produce, so they were relatively more scarce and more valuable than in later industrial societies. Taken together, a household's textile items—clothing, bed and table linens, towels and sacks, wall coverings and cushions, rope and twine—could account for as much as one-fourth of the value of all household goods. Some cloth was produced locally for local consumption, with all the processes done "at home," from growing the raw material through producing the thread to weaving the cloth. But as the fourteenth century progressed, more aspects of cloth production were becoming full-time trades. Across England a complex network of producers, brokers, and retailers moved textile goods from one stage to the next. This increasing organization and industrialization enabled England, once primarily an exporter of raw wool, to develop into an important producer of woolen cloth. But imported textiles such as silk brocades and cotton wool remained high-priced luxury goods.

To make woolen cloth, the wool was sheared from the sheep, carded to untangle and straighten the fibers, and spun into thread. Much thread was still produced on traditional drop spindles; although the new "great wheels" were making the spinning process easier, faster, and more consistent, they were expensive and still somewhat limited in the types of thread they could produce. Finally, the thread was woven into cloth on looms.

To make linen or hemp cloth, flax or hemp plants were taken up roots and all, and retted (soaked) to soften them. After washing and drying they were beaten to break down the outer layers, which were scraped off with wooden scutching knives. The inner fibers were combed with a heckle to the desired fineness. The finer threads were spun into linen thread; the leftover material or herds was also spun, and used for the coarser fabric called herden.

Some fabrics required additional specialized processes. Wool cloth might be fulled (beaten or trodden in water) to thicken it by shrinking the loose fibers, and then stretched on tenters (long wooden frames with hooks to hold the cloth as it dried). Either wool or linen could be dyed, perhaps following lengthy, complex recipes, but linen was usually just bleached, as it is easy to bleach but hard to dye. The surface of wool cloth might be teaseled (brushed) to raise its nap, or sheared to refine its texture. The many crafts involved in making and selling textiles remain with us today in the surnames derived from them, such as Shearer, Fuller, Dyer, Weaver, Taylor, Mercer, and Draper.

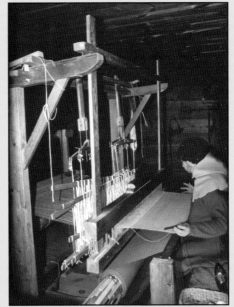

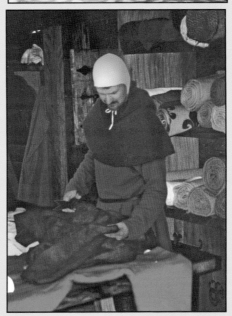

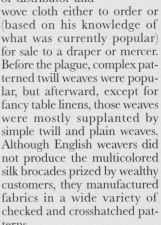

A weaver obtained purpose-spun threads from a producer or distributor and wove cloth either to order or (based on his knowledge of what was currently popular) for sale to a draper or mercer. Before the plague, complex patterned twill weaves were popular, but afterward, except for fancy table linens, those weaves were mostly supplanted by simple twill and plain weaves. Although English weavers did not produce the multicolored silk brocades prized by wealthy customers, they manufactured fabrics in a wide variety of checked and crosshatched patterns.

A dyer worked on either unwoven threads (for sewing or braiding, or for use in patterned weaving) or finished cloth. Colors rose and fell in popularity, and recipes for fashionable shades were closely guarded. In general, deeper shades were more expensive because of the added time and dyestuff required to achieve them, but high-demand or hard to achieve shades could also be costly.

Tailors made garments to order or for off-the-rack sale. Cutting patterns were as yet unknown, but the craft of tailoring had been developing rapidly over the previous decades. Innovations such as the set-in sleeve produced garments that were not only more flattering but also more practical. Innovations in lacing and the use of buttons permitted closer, more elegant silhouettes. But styles and techniques percolated through society fairly slowly; while the nobility and wealthy commoners might be up to date, townspeople tended to lag a bit, and country folk often clung to the styles of their parents' or grandparents' days.

Gilbert Mercer is Dunbury's hayward, responsible for overseeing the agricultural work of the manor. Here he stops by to check on the progress of two tenants, Thomas Stockbridge and John Arundel.

John Arundel is hammering a replacement tine into the harrow, while Thomas Stockbridge whittles another. Repairing the harrow is the last item on a long list of repairs they have had to make over the winter months, when the days were short and cold and nothing was growing.

Now the first hints of spring fill them with a new sense of urgency. They must make sure that everything they will need is ready. The plow and the harrow must be ready to take to the fields. The billhooks, sickles, scythes, hatchets, and axes must be sharp. All of the pails and buckets must be tight and secure. New shovels must be cut from wood and shod with iron, and mauls checked to ensure that their iron banding has kept the heads strong through the dryness of winter. The manor's cart must be in good repair and the leather of the horse harnesses checked to ensure that it is strong and supple. All this and more besides must be cleaned, repaired, and ready for the new season.

Soon the manor folk's attention will turn to planting the spring crops. When the weather warms and the ground is thawed, the plowmen will be out to plow and harrow the fields. Men and women will break up stubborn clods of earth with mauls. When the fields are ready, the spring crops of barley, oats, and legumes will be sown, then the fields will be harrowed again to cover the seed. The seed must be in the ground by the end of March to maximize the growing season.

Eyes also search for signs of the year's first grain—wheat, planted after the harvest. Soon it will begin to sprout.

Sir Geoffrey's woodlands are managed as carefully as his food crops. His woodmen tend them, encouraging them to produce the most useful balance of timber and wood. "Timber" refers to the big trunks of trees, used to frame houses and other buildings and to make planks and beams. "Wood" is of smaller diameter—poles and rods used for firewood, fencing, and lighter construction—and may be either underwood (from the trunks of smaller trees) or the branches of timber trees. The woodland at Dunbury manor is a mix of timber trees (sometimes called standards) and underwood.

Most of Sir Geoffrey's underwood is produced by coppicing, growing from the stump of a tree. Once a tree is cut, its stump quickly sends up springs (new shoots); within five to eight years they grow into straight, well-shaped rods and poles that can be harvested, and the process is begun again. Each year the woodmen harvest only a portion of the underwood so that there is a constant supply of springs. Some springs are allowed to grow into trees, a process called suckering.

The standards are cut down as needed, usually when they are between twenty-five and a hundred years old. Timber trees are selected for felling by the carpenter, to ensure that they meet his needs. He selects timber at the desired size instead of cutting it to size, and then—if he is building a house—fits the construction around the natural shape of the tree. Taking advantage of wood's natural configuration reduces the need to cut and join pieces, and results in a stronger frame.

Cattle, sheep, and deer are a challenge to woodmen because they like to eat the young shoots of trees. Sometimes, rather than coppicing, the woodmen pollard a tree or stand of trees, cutting them six to fifteen feet above the ground. The springs grow from the resulting bolling (permanent trunk), above the reach of the hungry animals.

Sir Geoffrey's woods are mostly coppiced standards and underwood, surrounded by a bank of earth and a ditch combined with fences and hedges that mark the boundaries and protect the woods from grazing animals. Gates allow the woodmen access to the woods; tenant access is closely regulated.

As the weather improves, Sir Geoffrey decides that it is past time for the boys among his fosterlings (children of gentle birth being raised in his household) to get in some martial practice. Among the boys currently at Dunbury, only John Peel and Edward Upham are over fourteen, the age at which it is suitable to begin learning the skills of arms. John is Sir Geoffrey's nephew, and Edward is his godson, the son of his old friend Lionel Upham. Their families have sent them to the Peels to learn the skills and accomplishments proper to a knight.

Remembering how eager he was when he was their age, he doubts that they will find the exercise a hardship. The knight wears his padded gambeson, the garment he would wear beneath his metal armor. The fast-growing boys no longer fit in last year's gambesons and the new ones are not yet finished, so they wear their everyday clothes. As Sir Geoffrey expects, Edward (in the green tunic) and John (in the red) are anxious to get started.

The lads begin their day practicing light sword strokes against the pell, a wooden target about man-height—in this case an old tree. Sir Geoffrey watches them closely, advising them on how to control their weapons. Striking a sword against a solid target such as a wooden post can ruin the weapon, but developing an understanding of how a sword moves is vital to fencing. Once Sir Geoffrey is satisfied that they understand the basics, he will switch them to wooden practice swords and teach them how to generate power for their strikes, letting them smite the pell mightily until their arms are sore.

Sir Geoffrey demonstrates how, after catching John's sword stroke on his blade, he can use a simple elbow push to expose John to his sword point. Then he shows that he need not kill an opponent caught this way, and uses a wrestling move to throw John to the ground.

Having shown the lads how effective the technique is, Sir Geoffrey instructs them in the proper placement of their hands and feet. Once he is satisfied that they understand the basics, he will let them practice on each other to learn the technique.

Basic skills for the joust are first learned on foot. John runs at the quintain, a tool for learning to use a lance. He tries to put the point within the horseshoe nailed to the board. As the lance hits, the pole with the target rotates. Edward is holding the sand-filled bag whose weight creates resistance when the target is hit. He will release it as the lance point strikes.

The lads must learn how to receive a lance strike and how to use a shield to deflect the point. John sits on a stool and Edward runs at him. To make things a little safer while they are learning, John wears a jousting helm and Edward's lance point has been removed.

The boys must also learn how to put on a knight's armor. Both are wearing mail shirts. Edward supports the weight of his breastplate as John fastens the straps that will hold it in place. Armor is heavy and restricts movement. The lads must get used to carrying that weight, and learn how the armor changes the way they move. Their lives may depend on it.

When the training is done for the day, the boys must take care of their equipment. Here, they have put their mail shirts into barrels, along with some sand and a little vinegar, and are rolling the barrels to clean the shirts. Pushing the barrels uphill takes some muscle, but John has an easier way to get them back down the hill.

A gentry woman's typical day begins early, with Mass and private devotions. After breakfast, she meets with the heads of the household offices to review the day's tasks, settle disputes, and make necessary decisions. The workings of the house tend to be divided between male and female domains. The hall, chamber, kitchen, chapel, and stables are managed by men and the senior officers are all male, although many wives work alongside their husbands (as Ursula Doughty does in the kitchen) or elsewhere in the household. Lady Joan's province is primarily the children and her own attendants, but over time she has taken on increasing responsibility for overseeing the day-to-day activities of the main departments. She was taught as a girl to read, write, and do simple arithmetic, and she can reckon well enough to periodically audit the various departments' accounts. If Sir Geoffrey decides to accept Sir John Stratton's indenture, Lady Joan will be responsible for all the household and estate management in his absence, and her knowledge of the household's operations will serve her in good stead.

At dinner there may be guests; Lady Joan welcomes the break in Dunbury's usual quiet isolation. Afterward she spends most of the afternoon in the solar (private upstairs room) with her women. Here they sit at the daily sewing—a continual necessity for women of all but the highest rank. She and Dame Katherine are joined by another fosterling, Rose Wilkin, a daughter of one of Lady Joan's friends from her days in service to the Countess of Pembroke. Dame Katherine has been instructing Rose in plain sewing, and now she pauses in her mending to inspect an almost-finished shirt. Lady Joan is transferring a set of buttons to her checked gown. Marjorie atte Well searches her embroidery threads for a particular color. Marjorie is the daughter of an embroiderer in Southampton, an associate of the le Flemyngs; she and Dionisia Lene do much of the household's embroidery. Dionisia is working on Sir Geoffrey's new second-best gown, enriching its somber blackness with silk scrolls and leaves at the shoulders. This is an opportunity for Lady Joan to instruct Rose in the duties and behavior of a gentlewoman,

and to monitor and instruct the women who serve her. But it is also a time for light amusements: exchanging news and gossip, telling stories, singing, and playing with Katherine's baby daughter Cecily.

Lady Joan is both pious and educated, so she follows the fashion of praying the Hours, an abbreviated version of the Divine Office recited by members of religious orders. She has a small Book of Hours containing the Little Office of the Virgin Mary, which focuses on the life and virtues of the Blessed Virgin. The great nobles can commission lavish Books of Hours with magnificent paintings and gilding; Lady Joan's is far less extravagant, with only a few small pictures and a

bit of rubrication (red lettering). As sunset nears, Lady Joan will read the prayers for Vespers with her women, in the solar or the chapel. After a modest supper, she may spend some time in the hall with Sir Geoffrey and the family, playing chess or tables (a backgammon-like game), or listening to stories or music. Finally she will retire to the chamber, where she may read for a while before the prayers of Compline and then bed.

Throughout the year, the faithful engage in a variety of religious observations, ranging from formal liturgies to informal personal practices.

Father Paul hears Lady Joan's confession. Like many pious people, she hears Mass often—in her case, daily—but rarely receives the Eucharist. The risk of receiving the sacrament in a state of sin is more frightening than the potential for grace is comforting. With Easter approaching, she has begun giving more than usual attention to her regular confessions to prepare for the required annual Eucharist. Father Paul refers to guidebooks called penitentials to help direct her in examining her conscience.

Their chief concern is whether Lady Joan has succumbed to any of the Seven Deadly Sins (pride, envy, gluttony, lust, wrath, avarice, sloth) or their lesser variants. The penance assigned to a sinner is determined by considerations such as the gravity of the sin, the circumstances of its commission, the sinner's motives, and the depth of the sinner's contrition. Penances can vary in severity and duration and include prayer, fasting, almsgiving, making restitution, pilgrimage, or even retiring to a religious house.

Julian Wallis tells her beads, using a length of wooden beads to keep track of each *Pater Noster* (Our Father) and *Ave Maria* (Hail Mary). This practice has not yet become codified as the Rosary, a systematized devotion to and meditation on the Blessed Virgin.

William Cressy's man Daniel Dalroun stops to pray at a roadside shrine, a wooden crucifix sheltered under a simple roof. This sort of shrine is more common on the Continent, but some of the Peels' Flemish connections introduced them to it, and the manor folk have taken to it.

Sir Geoffrey's tenants at Dunbury are free men and women, but most tenants on St. Mary's nearby manors are villeins: unfree, bound to the land and obligated to work it to their lord's benefit; they owe varying sorts of goods and services to the lord. Some are customary labor, enshrined in ancient traditions, and others are part of the fees owed by the villein. Free tenants have arrangements specifying the money and few remaining services, which they owe to Sir Geoffrey in return for the land they occupy and work. They have rights and privileges (such as access to the royal court system) not given to villeins.

Even before the Death the Peels, like many knightly landlords, had found it increasingly hard to get enough villein labor to work the demesne land (the portion of the manor that they cultivate directly, rather than renting). Over the years, they have converted most of the demesne land to rental and allowed free tenants to rent additional lands. By now families that once were villeins hold their parcels in free tenure. The cash income relieves Sir Geoffrey of some of the ups and downs of agricultural earnings, and permits him to pay for more services in cash. At Dunbury there are three plowmen (sometimes more, hired for the season), shepherds for the various flocks, a cowherd (although Sir Geoffrey keeps few cattle), a swineherd, a dairymaid, a keeper of the cheese, a beer keeper, a cellarer, and a keeper of the grain in the fields. None of these jobs are full-time, or pay enough to live on; one person may hold more than one of them, or supplement wages with farming or craft work. Many tenants take on seasonal work for a little extra cash.

John Arundel holds one virgate (about forty acres), half of another, and a four-acre parcel, and pays thirty-two shillings a year.

Thomas Stockbridge holds a quarter-virgate messuage (house with associated land) and smaller parcels of two, five, and eight acres, and pays fourteen shillings a year.

The Spryngots, a prosperous tenant family, have steadily expanded their holdings since the Great Pestilence. Among them they now hold five virgates and fifty acres of demesne land; for the demesne land they pay thirty shillings a year, and for the remainder one hundred. Richard Spryngot (called Hick) and his brothers are determined to advance the family's status and wealth, and as individuals and as a group they continually seek out opportunities to increase their income and assets.

On Dunbury manor, the most important official is the bailiff. He is responsible for the general management of the manor; he must see to the preparation of the accounts and ensure good returns on the manor's resources. On some manors the bailiff is an outsider, but Sir Geoffrey prefers to appoint a local man, who knows the manor and has ties to the land and the other tenants. While this means a bailiff with knowledge of the manor folk and the manorial customs, it also means that the chosen man must constantly balance his loyalties between his lord and his fellows.

James Warde is Dunbury's bailiff. Though not the ablest of men, he is well liked, doubtless due in part to his tendency to let the tenants do as they will. He manages to buy and sell well enough, but he tends to leave many of his duties to the hayward of the manor, while he harbors dreams of improving his status, primarily though military achievements.

This year's hayward at Dunbury is Gilbert Mercer. Unlike the bailiff, the hayward is elected by the tenants (subject to Sir Geoffrey's approval). Gilbert has served many times before, and has held the position for the last seven years. He is an active and sharp man, who watches carefully and patrols late and early to look after the crops in the fields. He supervises the plowing, harrowing, sowing, mowing, reaping, and gathering, and is generally attentive for the manor's wellbeing.

Other manorial officials elected by the tenants include woodwards and foresters, responsible for Sir Geoffrey's woods, and ale-tasters, who enforce quality regulations.

Trouble is brewing on the manor as Thomas Stockbridge confronts John Arundel. It seems that pigs have strayed into Thomas's field, causing a good deal of damage to the young crop. Thomas asserts that it was John's pigs that made the mischief. John tries to dismiss the trespass, claiming it was must have been someone else's pigs.

Thomas is highly unsatisfied with John's response and takes his complaint to the hayward. Gilbert does his best to calm the man down, but the damage to his crop cannot be undone.

Gilbert does not like being caught in the middle of the argument. He also does not wish to tell Sir Geoffrey that his tenants are quarreling. In hopes of finding an amicable solution to the problems, he speaks with John. John assures Gilbert that if his pigs had been responsible—which they certainly were not—he would willingly pay Thomas for the damage.

Sometimes it seems that there is little to the agricultural year beyond the harvest and everything leading up to it. For without all the hard work preparing for the harvest, there is no harvest—and everyone goes hungry.

In late spring, work becomes heavier and more intense, as more crops require attention and the livestock become more demanding. As soon as the ground has thawed, laborers plow and plant the spring crops of barley and legumes and a few oats. At the same time, the village women begin work in their household gardens. The fields that have been planted must be continually tended. Lambs and calves are being weaned, so dairying work begins as well.

The plow gets a lot of abuse as it is dragged through the sometimes rocky soil. The only metal parts on the plow are the coulter (a smaller blade that slices the soil vertically) and the plowshare (the larger blade that makes the actual furrow). The rest of the plow is made of wood, which gives it the necessary flexibility to cope with rocks and hard clots of earth, but also means that the joints easily work loose and must be tightened when they do. Hick Springot's plow is pulled by a team of eight oxen, but in some cases the job can be done by as few as four.

Whenever possible, crops are planted closely enough to choke out weeds, but sometimes there is nothing to do but go after the weeds one by one. Hick and his wife, Elena, prepare to do just that. Each has a pair of weeding sticks long enough that they can reach the ground without bending over. One stick has a forked end, used to tease out and hold the unwanted plant so that the other stick, with its hooked knife, can cut the weed at ground level.

Religious restrictions dramatically affect diet throughout the year. In England, eating meat, poultry, eggs, and dairy products is prohibited on Fridays and Saturdays (although many folk are lax about Saturdays), and sometimes on Wednesdays or the eves of important holy days. These are known as days of abstinence, or "fish days." During the liturgical season of Lent (the forty days leading up to Easter) abstinence is required every day except Sunday. During Lent the faithful must fast as well, restricting the number and size of meals.

Since food resources are already sparse at this time of year, the Lenten restrictions have relatively little effect on most tenants: the grain crops are still young, few fresh vegetables are in season, and the fruit crops are far from ripe. Everyone, even Sir Geoffrey's household, relies on preserved foods. Only the grain that was stored away from the last harvest is available for making bread or porridge. Dried fruits and stored root vegetables can be had from the larder, but each day the stocks diminish. Since the dairy herd is yielding very little, the forbidden cheese, milk, and butter are scarce anyway.

But for some folk, various exemptions and exceptions—or ready cash—can make the Lenten discipline less onerous.

Gilbert Mercer's meal for this Lenten day is a bowl of gruel, a mix of dried grains, peas, and beans cooked in water. Sometimes ale replaces the water, but even then the gruel remains a flavorless, though nourishing, meal. For commoners, food during Lent is boring and repetitive: pottages, gruels, and stews. The assortment of grains, root vegetables, and occasional dried fruits may change, but the sameness of it all is wearying.

Sir Geoffrey and his household get a more varied diet. Fresh fish are available from the river and local ponds, as long as the waters are not frozen over, and seafood such as mussels and lobsters as well as sea fishes such as herring and cod are brought up from Southampton. His well-trained cook, Philip Doughty, makes the most of the monotonous foodstuffs by cooking them in different ways, changing the consistency and flavor, and adding spicy or pungent sauces to keep Lady Joan satisfied. And although the number and size of meals are restricted, Sir Geoffrey and his family suffer little from this: collations (snacks or light meals) are a common way to dodge the restriction on actual meals.

Persons expected to perform heavy manual labor need to keep up their strength. By practical necessity, the restrictions of Lent are lightened for them. They are allowed to eat eggs and dairy products such as the cheese that Thomas Stockbridge is enjoying before a day of plowing.

Such practicality extends to the elderly, the very young, and the sick as well. All have the Church's dispensation to eat restricted foods.

Sir Brian du Bois, steward of Sir Geoffrey's large manor at Brockhurst, has ridden in to confer with him. The growing season is underway, but there are many matters of concern for the coming year, especially since Sir Geoffrey has agreed to Sir John Stratton's proposal. There are ditches to be cleared, banks to be rebuilt, hedges and fences to be mended, and buildings to be repaired at both properties. Sir Brian reports that the ewe-houses at Brockhurst need new roofs. It is not a cost Sir Geoffrey wants to add to the long list of expenses, but it must be done for the health of the flock. When they reach the mill, it is apparent to both knights that the mill pond needs cleaning. More expense.

As important as this inspection may be, the knights find their conversation turning more to matters in the wider world. The earl of Buckingham's army remains in Brittany and a new poll tax has been proclaimed to help pay the expenses. Unlike the previous tax, this one was not graduated by means and rank, and every person above the age of fifteen is expected to pay twelve pence. It is a trivial sum to Sir Geoffrey, but the burden on his tenants is great, triple that of the previous tax. Already there is much grumbling among the commoners. Sir Geoffrey wants no disruptions on his manors this year, so the knights discuss ways to help out the poorer tenants as the tax law enjoins them to do.

Sir Geoffrey's plans to gather a military company raise important issues about the supervision of Dunbury and the other Peel properties in his absence. Lady Joan can manage them with the help of a good staff, but can Sir Brian—eager to make his name in France—be spared? Who could serve in his stead?

There are strictly military questions to be considered as well. The company will not depart for several months, because there is much to prepare; troops must be recruited and trained, and transport arranged to Bordeaux and beyond. How many troops can be raised from among the tenants and still leave the Peel properties in good order? How many men must be hired elsewhere? How best to put about the word that Sir Geoffrey is recruiting?

And what of the talk that a new army may go to France, led by the king? Sir Geoffrey's agreement with Sir John Stratton will be nullified if the king calls for men to follow him. What would be the prospects of such a campaign? The war in France has not been going well, and the last few years have seen the French bold enough to raid England. Dunbury is some distance from the coast, but will those left behind be safe?

The two men ride on deep in discussion, questions of husbandry and warfare intermingling.

SUMMER

Easter, the heart of the religious year, is a movable feast: it falls on the first Sunday after the first full moon after the spring equinox. This year it comes on the fourteenth day of April, and after the privations of Lent and the heightened rigors of Holy Week (the week before Easter), the feast day itself provides a welcome break from agricultural labors and an opportunity to enjoy some of the early spring produce.

Easter also marks the start of summer, by agricultural reckoning. Labor never stops, but it is easier in April and May. The crops must still be vigilantly weeded and the fallow fields are plowed one or more times to prepare them for being brought back into productivity.

Not all land is equally suited to all grain crops. Wheat, for example, can only be grown in well-manured, well-drained fields. Sir Geoffrey maintains a storage barn for his corn (the leading crop of an area, in Dunbury's case wheat). He can sell this stored corn when necessary, sometimes to his own tenants.

In June, before Midsummer's Day, the manor's sheep will be driven to streams and washed before the shearing. This is important work and involves most of the men and women of the manor, some working with their own flocks and others hired to help with Sir Geoffrey's.

At the end of June the grass in the meadows will have grown high, and it will be time to make hay. The manor folk will turn out again, the men cutting the stalks with scythes and the women and children following behind to gather the cuttings into sheaves. After the sheaves have dried and been taken to storage, livestock will be driven out into the meadows to graze on the stubble.

On a morning in early summer, Gilbert Mercer and John Arundel discuss the state of the crops as they watch other men head out to work in the fields. They stand beside Sir Geoffrey's fishpond. Fish and seafood are an important part of everyone's diet, and not just during Lent. Rivers, ponds, and lakes provide eels, crayfish, and freshwater fish such as trout, perch, tench, and carp. Coastal waterways, bays, and the sea supply mussels, cockles, lobsters, and sea fish. Most are caught wild, but some are farmed. Fish farming in ponds and rivers is practiced on many manors to provide a ready source of fresh fish throughout the year. Dunbury's three ponds are a valuable source of pike and eel for the many fish days. The fish in the manor's ponds and waterways, like the beasts of field and forest, are the lord's property. Although it is a crime to take a fish from any of the ponds without Sir Geoffrey's permission, manor folk sometimes attempt it by night.

Stephen Wallis has obtained permission from the Peels and the bishop to go on pilgrimage to Canterbury, the shrine of the martyred saint Thomas Becket. He must be back by the Feast of the Ascension, forty days after Easter, so he will make the round trip (about 260 miles) as quickly as possible.

Stephen will join the main route to Canterbury at Stockbridge, a few miles downstream of Dunbury where the Salisbury-Winchester road crosses the Test. He expects to find other pilgrims there, with whom he can travel for fellowship and protection. He can pack lightly compared to pilgrims bound for Rome or the Holy Land, but he has been careful to bring the most commonly recommended items: a warm gown, cooking and eating gear, a dagger, needle and thread and thimble, extra braes and points, and snacks of nuts and dried fruits.

Stephen's fellow servants and friends, eager to share in the spiritual benefits he will gain, have given him offerings to take to the shrine. He will buy inexpensive tokens in Canterbury, have them blessed in the Cathedral, and bring them back to Dunbury where they will be prized as relics of St. Thomas.

Pilgrimage is a popular devotional activity among those who can afford it. People go on pilgrimage to offer thanks for answered prayers, do penance for sins, or increase in grace through proximity to holy relics. In addition, pilgrimage offers all the attractions of leisure travel—freedom from daily responsibilities, new sights and people, and adventure. Lively commercial centers have sprung up around the most popular destinations, offering food, lodging, and souvenirs.

In England, the most popular pilgrimage sites are Canterbury and Walsingham, but many churches and shrines attract smaller or more seasonal numbers. Beyond the sea there are likewise many pilgrimage sites of different size and popularity; the three main destinations are Jerusalem and Rome, each with many devotional sites, and the shrine of St. James the Greater at Compostela in northwestern Spain.

The central act of a pilgrimage was usually some kind of contact with relics of the saint or saints honored at the site. Pilgrims gained grace through seeing or touching a portion of the saint's own body, or some object associated with the saint in life. Since many people were unable to make a pilgrimage, those who did sought ways to enable the folks at home to share in the benefits. One popular way was by purchasing signs such as cast lead images, which the pilgrim would touch to the relic or have blessed in the shrine, then give to the home-bound ones on his return, enabling them to receive some of the grace of the pilgrimage.

Chaucer's greatest work, the Canterbury Tales, is organized around a trip to Canterbury by a diverse group of pilgrims representing common "types" in contemporary English society, among them a respectable ship captain, a strapping yeoman, a rowdy miller, and an adventurous widow.

The traditional gear of a pilgrim to the shrine of St. James at Compostela comprised a hat with a cockleshell (the symbol of the shrine), cloak, scrip (satchel), and knobbed staff. Over time, this costume came to designate any pilgrim, regardless of destination.

A heap of lead pilgrim signs, depicting the head of St. Thomas Becket, lie ready to have their casting residue removed. To their left is the three-part stone mold used to produce them. The mold needs three parts so that the pin and clasp can be cast as part of the badge.

The law of the land requires each man to practice archery on Sunday. Since everyone gathers for Mass on Sunday, it is convenient to practice in the churchyard afterward.

It takes years to develop the strength to pull the great war bows, and much practice is needed before an archer has the skill to nock an arrow, aim while drawing, and loose cleanly so that the arrow flies straight and true to the target. Yet Sunday practice is often more a social gathering than a serious attempt to improve archery skills. Of course the men do become more serious about it when there is a threat of invasion from the French or the possibility of other military action.

Some of the men from the manor and village have gathered in the parish church yard. Hick Spryngot, the manor's best archer and Sir Geoffrey's sometimes huntsman, leads the practice.

Most of the men have bows of yew, widely considered the best wood for the purpose. But other woods are used as well, including ash, elm, and wych (a variety of elm).

Once the men have had their go, John Arundel watches proudly as his son Tomkyn gets his first lesson from Hick Spryngot. Young John, bored and unable to participate, competes for his father's attention.

Tomkyn holds out a stick at arm's length for as long as he can, to build his arm strength. Soon he will get a bow, which—like the men's—will be a handspan longer than his height and suited to his strength. As he grows and improves, he will move on to bigger and stronger bows.

Hick demonstrates a method for stringing the bow. This one requires a lot of arm and upper body strength, which all archers must develop.

On the first day of May, Sir Geoffrey and his household have ridden out into the country to celebrate the season and bring home garlands and branches of the new growth. They observe the tradition of wearing green in honor of the new life springing in the countryside. Lady Joan and her women sit in a meadow enjoying the pleasant, warm day; they pick wildflowers and weave garlands and wreaths from daisies (beloved of lovers, a symbol of young love and the transience of beauty) and greenery (signifying faithful love and constancy). In courtly circles, the debate between Flower and Leaf has been developed into an elaborate game of "allegiance" to one or the other, but at Dunbury the celebration is far simpler.

The party strolls along the old Saxon dike, once a barrier to deer but now weathered to a pleasant raised walkway across the countryside. Young John Peel and Edward Upham have run on ahead to where the picnic awaits. Lady Joan adjusts Sir Geoffrey's garland, the badge of his allegiance to the party of the flower. Dame Katherine and Rose Wilkin, leaders of the party of the leaf, laugh as they sing the old song

> *En mai, quant rose est florie*
> *Que j'oi ces oisiaus chanter*
> *Moi covient par druerie*
> *Joie demener.*

(In May, when the rose is blooming and I hear the birds singing, I like however I can to seek for joy.)

Near the end of May, Sir Geoffrey enjoys a hunt. Though it has a real value in bringing back food for the larder, this excursion is primarily a social occasion. The knight sits at a well-laid table with William Cressy and James Warde. Hick Spryngot, in his role as huntsman, has brought some fewmets (deer droppings), carried in his horn from where he found them in the forest. The men scrutinize the fewmets to judge the quality of their prey.

Stephen Wallis, back from Canterbury, tends the gaze-hounds (dogs that hunt by sight rather than by scent) who will soon be set to coursing the deer, driving them until the hunters dispatch them. Young John Peel, unhappy that James Warde's presence has relegated him to a cloth on the ground with the bailiff's sons, longs for the action of the hunt proper. Gilbert Mercer, William's man Daniel Dalroun, and several tenants, hired for the day as huntsmen, are content to enjoy the food Sir Geoffrey provides and the holiday atmosphere of this welcome break from their ordinary labors.

ᗱunting by tenants is, on the whole, forbidden. Pests such as wolves or moles can be killed, often with a reward from Sir Geoffrey for doing so, but game animals are for the knight's hunting. Manor folk who poach will be fined, although this does not deter all of them. Hick Spryngot is hunting deer—not for himself but for Sir Geoffrey's table.

Small birds are not reserved to Sir Geoffrey and are welcome sources of meat for the manor folk. Birds can be caught from the trees with nets affixed to long poles or with snares among the bushes.

Gilbert Mercer attempts to muzzle a wriggling ferret. As hayward he is responsible for keeping pests from damaging the crops. Since they were brought to England after the Conquest, coneys have spread far and wide. Although the coneys in Sir Geoffrey's warrens are restricted to the Peels' use, they often escape, becoming a pest to crops and a distraction to hunting dogs. Gilbert will lead a group of tenants and dogs in chasing the coneys into the warren, the maze of burrows in which they live. When the coneys have gone to ground, the men will block all known entrances or cover them with nets. Once the ferret is muzzled—lest it kill and eat the coneys within the burrow—Gilbert will release it into the warren. The frightened coneys will race into the nets and be caught.

But all this is done under strict oversight: anyone caught poaching the lord's coneys (or his deer or fish) is subject to substantial fines.

At Dunbury, animals of several kinds share the land with the people. Sir Geoffrey's land supports hundreds of sheep, and small flocks of chickens and other birds. There are also horses, a few cattle, and many hogs. Any of these can end up in Sir Geoffrey's larder or be put up for sale.

Tenants are allowed their own animals as well. Most of them keep poultry, a few pigs, some sheep, and perhaps a cow. A few keep oxen or horses for plowing and haulage. The more prosperous tenant families like the Spryngots and Mercers have substantial flocks of sheep.

Tenants can pay to put their hogs in Sir Geoffrey's woods to eat the mast there and dig for tubers and roots. For another fee, they can put their hogs in his stubble fields. Most often the pigs are simply left on their own to root for sustenance—and sometimes they stray where they are not wanted. Thomas Stockbridge and John Arundel are still wrangling over the crop damage done by pigs back in the spring.

The land around Dunbury is not the best for horses. Sir Geoffrey has a small herd here, and each year a few foals (such as the one Gilbert Mercer watches, trying to judge its strength as it hides behind its mother) are born to the breeding mares. But Sir Geoffrey maintains his primary breeding stock at his manor in Brockhurst, where the grazing is better and Sir Brian du Bois takes a special interest in their welfare. Although the horses suffice to supply his riding, haulage, and military needs, the animals are not of exceptional quality; Sir Geoffrey is not as interested in horses as his grandfather was.

Oxen are still used by many of the tenants for plowing and other heavy draft work, and are favored over horses since they are more economical to keep and, when too old to work, can be fattened and slaughtered for food.

Cows can provide milk for most of the year, although the yield and value vary dramatically. A cow in full milk can yield up to four times as much as at other times. Milk is scarce in winter and may sell for as much as three times its summer price. Fresh milk can be drunk, and the rich cream is a treat, but they are more important as the basis for cheese and butter.

The women of the tenant families are usually in charge of the cows, seeing to their needs as well as collecting the milk and making the butter and cheese.

Sheep and downland (such as Dunbury manor's lands) are made for each other. Since sheep—unlike cattle—do not require much water, the manor's streams and wells provide sufficient water for their needs. There is plenty of nutritious grass on the downs, where the chalky soil also curbs disease common in lower, damper lands.

All this is to Sir Geoffrey's liking, as sheep are valuable in many ways. Mutton (the meat of mature sheep) is a mainstay in the Peels' larder. Kebbs (weak or sickly sheep) can be sold to local butchers or stock dealers. Sheep manure is rich fertilizer, and as flocks are driven from one pasture to another tenants make sure to take advantage of any rights they have to pasture Sir Geoffrey's sheep on their fields. There is also minor income to be had from the sale of fells (skins), of butter and cheese made from sheep's milk, and from lactage payments for the rental of milking ewes. But the real money is in wool. English wool, renowned across Europe for its quality, commands a premium price, and wool sales provide nearly two-thirds of the earnings from Sir Geoffrey's flocks.

Sir Geoffrey's lands sustain several sorts of flocks. The ewe flock at Dunbury, with its breeding females and nursing lambs, is basic to the balance of all the flocks. The other principal flock is made up of wethers (castrated males), which yield the heaviest fleeces. Flock size and makeup are managed by transferring sheep between flocks. For example, the wether flock is regularly enlarged with lambs moved from the ewe flock, or bought in the market. Occasionally surplus hoggasters (young sheep) are sent to other manors, to be fattened for slaughter or to strengthen the flocks there.

Within the greater agricultural year, sheep farming has its own seasons. Lambing time is in early spring before the spring sowing. Adult sheep are sheared in mid-June and the fleeces carted to market. A single fleece will weigh between one and two pounds, and be valued between two and eight pence. The finest English wool, from long-fleeced sheep grown in the Midlands, can command up to sixpence a pound, but Sir Geoffrey's sheep produce wool that is shorter, coarser, and therefore less valuable.

In total the Dunbury flocks comprise nearly 2000 head; the flocks at other manors range between 800 and 3000 head. In the pastures they are generally gathered into sheepfolds made of hurdles (portable fences of woven sticks), to protect them from predators, protect crops from them, control where they drop their valuable manure, and facilitate caring for their health.

A vigilant shepherd constantly watches for disease among his flock. Sir Geoffrey's flocks lose about one sheep in fifteen from disease, and kebbs are frequent. The most common complaints are murrain, scab, pox, and fluke. Geffrey Breton, who keeps the hoggaster flock, has several remedies at hand, primarily ointments with ingredients such as sulfur, tar, and verdigris. Here he brings a mixture of oil, tallow, and quicksilver for sheep-pox.

A wide variety of poultry is raised on the manor: chickens, geese, doves, swans, and peafowl. They provide meat and eggs, and feathers for stuffing pillows and fletching arrows. Sir Geoffrey keeps a large flock of geese and pays Tomkyn Arundel to watch them. The boy's hood is the only equipment he needs—both to herd the geese and to protect them if they are menaced by a bird of prey.

Most of the tenants keep a few chickens. Hens are a steady source of eggs, and occasionally a young male or old hen makes its way into the pot. Elisota Arundel is feeding her family's chickens. Like most women and girls on the manor, when her hands are not otherwise busy she uses the time to spin woolen thread. She carries a distaff with wool fiber and a spindle for spinning it into thread.

John and Agnes Everard gaze fondly at their first-born son in his cradle. Many noblewomen have little contact with their children, employing wet nurses, governesses, and tutors, but the Church encourages women to follow the example of the Blessed Virgin, who is often portrayed nursing the infant Jesus. Although the Everards are not noble, they can afford to hire a wet nurse; but Agnes nurses and cares for her son herself. With the help of a servant, she spends much of her time feeding and bathing the baby, changing swaddling, and comforting the yowling new addition to their family.

By contrast, Avis Arundel has no maid to help her. She has always nursed her babies herself, whether she likes it or not. She has carried infants with her and taken her young children along when she ran errands, worked about the house, or toiled in the field.

Although very young children are allowed a good deal of play time, by the age of four children are expected to begin contributing to the family, by caring for younger children, helping around the house and toft, and (in the case of girls) spinning wool and linen thread. Children are a valuable addition to a tenant family's resources and are put to work as soon as may be.

When the children of the gentry, especially boys, are old enough to leave their mothers, they may be fostered out to a family selected by their parents, preferably one of equal or higher station. This is done to further the child's and family's interests. Their parents, who love and cherish them, are apt to spoil them or provide too little discipline. Sending them to a foster family will ensure that the children learn more and are better reared, even if this means that they will be subject to stricter discipline and harsher punishments. It also strengthens alliances between families and improves prospects for later finding suitable spouses.

Literacy is becoming more and more important to the gentry, as society depends increasingly on written records. Most gentle men can read and write, many in more than one language; many gentle women can read, though fewer can write. Schooling from tutors is available for any free child whose parents can pay.

One reason the Peels have chosen Augustinian canons for their priests is the order's emphasis on educating the laity. Part of Father Alan's duties is to provide the gentry children with a basic education. The ambitious James Ward, who wishes to advance his family's status, pays Father Alan a fee to teach his son David because the Dunbury priest is too rarely in the village to operate a school.

Lessons start when the children are about seven years of age and continue until they are twelve or thirteen. Father Alan first sees to their religious training, and then teaches them to do basic arithmetic and to read and write Latin, French, and some English.

Students do much of their work from memory, but they also use wax tablets to take notes and work out exercises. Father Alan can check Edward Upton's wax tablet for any mistakes.

This sort of private education is not just for boys. Rose Wilkin attends the lessons so that she will be able to read her prayers and manage household accounts. Boy or girl, the basic education they receive from Father Alan will be useful when they come to manage estates of their own.

More formal schools are run by the Church primarily to prepare students for a life in Church service. Monastic schools are exclusively for potential monks and are one of the few places a boy from a poor family can get an education. Grammar schools, usually associated with a cathedral or other large church, have a broader curriculum than monastic schools, including the trivium (Latin grammar, rhetoric, and logic). The universities at Cambridge and Oxford offer intensive training in the trivium and the quadrivium (arithmetic, geometry, music, and astronomy) leading to the degree of Bachelor of Arts. More advanced curricula lead to degrees of Master of Arts or Doctor of Theology, Law, or Medicine. Students are accepted whenever they are deemed ready, and boys as young as thirteen attend.

In a small city or a town such as Southampton, craft guilds were far less structured or prominent than in London, but good training—and good connections—were still vitally important to a young man hoping to make a living as an artisan.

If a boy was accepted as an apprentice, he was bound to serve the master for a set period of time. How long depended on the trade and the local rules; it could be little as two years but was more commonly seven. From the master the lad received training in the skills necessary for the trade, gained insight into how business should be conducted, learned whatever else was necessary for business (such as doing sums and perhaps a little reading), and received moral guidance. The master was obliged to feed him and give him a place to sleep, likely in the shop or work space so that the apprentice could also serve as a watchman. The apprentice performed any tasks set for him by the master, usually beginning with unskilled, menial tasks such as fetching, carrying, and sweeping the floor. During this period, master and apprentice learned one another's temperament and abilities. After a time, the apprentice began to learn the trade, at first producing rough work that the master finished. He was subject to the master's discipline, up to and including beating for misbehavior or infractions of the master's rules.

By the time an apprentice completed his term, he was expected to be a fully capable craftsman, or journeyman (a man who is paid a daily wage, from the French *jour*, day). He might work for his original master or for another. If he had enough money saved up, he might try to set up his own shop, though in a town with a strong guild he usually had to be acknowledged as a master before doing so. Full and formal admission to a guild, sometimes after producing a "master work" to showcase his skills, was required before a man could call himself a master and take on apprentices of his own.

Master craftsmen were leading citizens in a town, and those in important and powerful guilds were the most prominent. Masters held many of the highest offices and, in some towns, controlled civic administration.

One of the le Flemyng servants brings his young son to a Southampton joiner, hoping that the boy will be accepted as an apprentice.

Elisota Arundel talks with Dobyn Taylor, son of Sir Geoffrey's woodward, at the gate to her father's toft. There is little chance for private chats in Dunbury village—the houses are small and thin-walled, and both of these young people are kept busy much of the time. But the village is small; they have known each other all their lives and see each other virtually every day. They have learned to take advantage of whatever moments arise.

Both families approve of the possible connection, but marriage is still a long way off. Royalty and nobility may wed very young, sometimes being nominally married as children, but this is because alliances need to be cemented and the ages of the principals are a minor consideration. For the common people, marriage usually happens much later, only after the man can establish a home and prove that he can support a family. Dunbury's tenants usually do not marry until well into their twenties.

Fortunately for young love, Dobyn's and Elisota's fathers are both free tenants; they will not need Sir Geoffrey's permission for a marriage, as they would if they were unfree. But by the custom of Dunbury manor, John and Avis will still have to pay a merchet (fee for a child's marriage), which will be no less than six pence.

In Southampton, the le Flemyngs have received horrifying news: rebels in London and the eastern counties have risen up against the royal administration, and a great mob has marched on London. Early reports are unclear as to their aims—do they truly seek an end to villeinage, the repeal of high rents and taxes, the breakup of Church estates, the abolition of lordship? Some rumors say that the rebels want to take the rule of England into their own hands, and be subject to no law but their own.

Then word comes that on the fourteenth of June the mob ran riot in London, murdering Archbishop Sudbury, the chancellor, and Sir Robert Hales, the king's treasurer, sacking and burning the duke of Lancaster's palace, releasing all prisoners from the Newgate and Fleet prisons, and even terrorizing the king's mother. Worse, from Master le Flemyng's point of view, dozens of foreigners were dragged from their houses and massacred in the streets, mostly Flemings like himself.

Discontent has been mounting around the town for months. What if the rebels come to Southampton? Master le Flemyng is not willing to stay and find out. None of his ships are in port, so he has no easy escape. Hastily he and his wife and the servants bundle together valuables and necessities, and head upriver toward Dunbury, where he will ask Sir Geoffrey to shelter them.

Once at Dunbury, they pour out their story to Sir Geoffrey. This is the first anyone on the manor has heard of the uprising, but Sir Geoffrey takes in the fugitives.

Over the next days and weeks they learn more. Mobs had indeed swarmed through Essex and Kent in the east, attacking monasteries and castles, destroying the houses of royal and local officials, killing some who opposed them and threatening others. A large contingent of rebels reached London and created havoc. But on the very day that the rebels killed the chancellor and treasurer, young King Richard, in a show of courage worthy of his father and grandfather, met with the rebels and their leader Wat Tyler. He listened to their grievances and granted many of their demands. The next day he met with them again, and the rebels made further demands. Somehow—the reports are conflicting—the rebel leader Tyler was killed, yet the king convinced the mob to leave London and disperse.

By the twenty-third of June forces loyal to the king, some under the command of the renowned soldier Sir Robert Knollys, rallied to Richard's support. Thus protected, the king cancelled the charters of freedom he had issued under duress and began the serious business of dealing with the lawless rebels. Sir Robert Passelewe and Sir Peter le Veel are sent into Hampshire and Wiltshire to repress any revolt they find. Sir Geoffrey is pleased to tell them that there has been no trouble at Dunbury.

By the end of the month, the le Flemyngs feel safe in returning home to Southampton. With fervent thanks, they set off down the river. Sir Geoffrey is pleased to have been of service—and to have Master le Flemyng indebted to him for his help.

Stephen of the hall is quite sure that the king has been poorly served by his advisors, especially in creating the last poll tax. The chancellor and treasurer paid for that folly, but they should rather have stood trial so that all could see their guilt. The lawlessness of the rebels troubles him. The world is meant to be ordered and each man is meant to know his place. To try to change that tempts God's punishment, and that of earthly lords as well, as the rebels have learned. Quite rightly.

Thomas Stockbridge thinks that the rebels made good sense. As he has heard said, when Adam delved and Eve span, who was then the gentleman? But the Garden of Eden was long ago and far away, and as the priests constantly remind him, man's state now is fallen and sinful. Men are men and will always seek advantage and advancement over other men: just look at the Spryngot family. There are gentlemen, and there are other men, and nothing is likely to change that. So why not just get on with the work that needs to be done?

Father Paul appreciates the difficulties that the king's taxes have brought, but the rebellion can only have been inspired by the devil. How can all men be equal under the king? Did not God create the three estates in their natural hierarchy? The rebels listened too much to the rogue preacher John Ball and too little to their honest parish priests. He has little doubt that many of the miscreants believe the false teachings of Wyclif and his followers as well. He resolves to pray for their misguided souls.

Pigs take little notice of human affairs, and the sun rises and sets every day whether men rise in rebellion or not. Tenants may talk among themselves about the right and wrong of the revolt but, as much as they might chafe at their lot in life, they know that Sir Geoffrey has been a better lord than many. Many of them saw the hard-eyed Sir Robert Passelewe and his men on their commission to suppress rebellion in Hampshire, and they have little doubt that the knights' swords would have been freely used on any Dunbury folk who had taken part in the uprising. Perhaps it is best to take a lesson from the pigs and just get on with life as it has always been.

Lady Joan directs the gardeners working in her pleasure garden. The manor's kitchen garden and orchard are elsewhere; here she grows flowers and herbs for delight rather than for practical use. They are planted in raised beds framed in wood, with graveled paths between. At one side stands the small stone base of a fountain, which will be installed as time and skills permit. The trellised fence encloses both the garden and a small herber, with trees and flowery turf, and sheltered seating from which to admire the view. In the background several of the tenants are building an arbor, on which Lady Joan plans to grow grape vines. This will provide a shaded, sweet-scented walk in the heat of the summer.

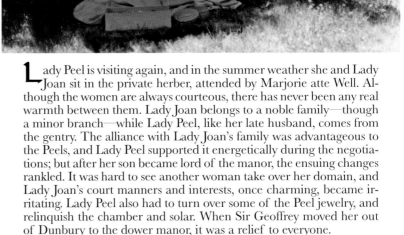

Lady Peel is visiting again, and in the summer weather she and Lady Joan sit in the private herber, attended by Marjorie atte Well. Although the women are always courteous, there has never been any real warmth between them. Lady Joan belongs to a noble family—though a minor branch—while Lady Peel, like her late husband, comes from the gentry. The alliance with Lady Joan's family was advantageous to the Peels, and Lady Peel supported it energetically during the negotiations; but after her son became lord of the manor, the ensuing changes rankled. It was hard to see another woman take over her domain, and Lady Joan's court manners and interests, once charming, became irritating. Lady Peel also had to turn over some of the Peel jewelry, and relinquish the chamber and solar. When Sir Geoffrey moved her out of Dunbury to the dower manor, it was a relief to everyone.

Lady Peel is partial to strawberries, and Lady Joan sends Marjorie to the kitchen with instructions to serve them at supper this evening.

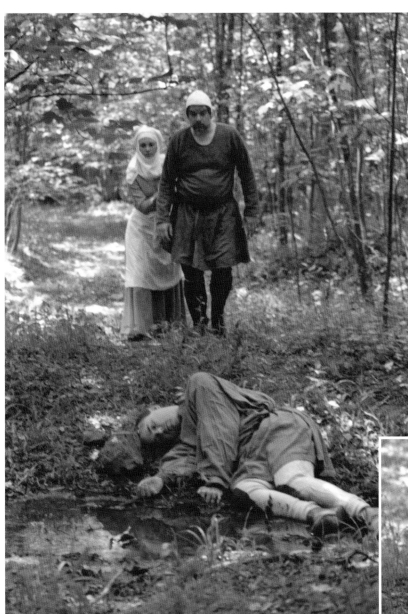

But Philip Doughty is not to be found in the kitchen. One of the kitchen servants tells Marjorie that he was visiting his ailing mother in the village. With time running short before the evening meal, Marjorie sets off to find Philip and see that he gets the message in time.

She finds Philip sooner than she expected. He lies unmoving beside one of the streams that cut though Sir Geoffrey's woods. Frightened, Marjorie runs for help. The first authority she happens upon is Gilbert Mercer. Now she leads him to where Philip lies.

Gilbert approaches cautiously. It is plain to him that Philip Doughty is dead: his head is broken and blood smears a stone on the ground beside him. Could someone have done murder on him? This will require official action. Gilbert must notify James Warde, who will appoint men to conduct an investigation and report to Sir Geoffrey. Gilbert sighs; as the first man on the scene, he can expect this added duty to land on him.

When the news reaches the manor house, Philip's wife Ursula is overcome. Julian Wallis hears the news and hurries to console her grieving friend.

Dunbury village boasts a flourishing shaw, a strip of controlled woodland between fields, where the small timber and wood that are in constant demand can be grown. It is also a good place for village boys to play a game of fox and hounds.

The game comes to a sudden end when a stranger appears on the road. He certainly is a big man, with the broad shoulders of an archer. Tomkyn Arundel, a budding archer himself, notes the arrow bag tucked under his belt and the cased bow over his shoulder. But more exciting, he has a hardened leather helmet on his head, and an aketon (padded cloth body armor) slung over his shoulder; the aketon bears a faded cross of St. George, a sign that he has served in the king's army. So he has been a soldier. His worn, ill-fitting clothing suggests that he may not have been a successful one.

Strangers are not common around Dunbury and the boys are too shy to speak to him. Instead they scurry off to spread word of his coming.

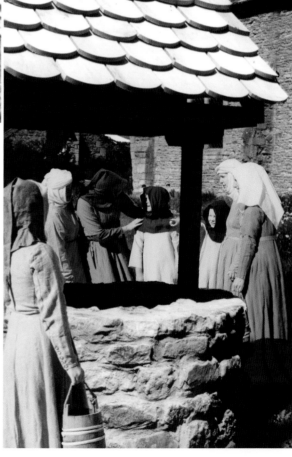

The boys find their mothers deep in gossip by the well. The women question the boys closely, and grow concerned at the news. There have been rumors of renewed rebellion in Kent. Could this stranger be bringing strife to the manor?

Avis Arundel recalls John's talk of joining Sir Geoffrey's company, and suggests that perhaps the man is simply a soldier come because he has heard that Sir Geoffrey is recruiting. Perhaps his tattered appearance is just the result of bad fortune.

The other women find this no great comfort. Archers are not just known for their skill with their bows; they are reputed to be brash, loud-mouthed, and great brawlers. And soldiers with no responsible person to command them are notorious troublemakers. What might this stranger bring to the village?

Sir Geoffrey and Sir Brian du Bois have decided that Sir Brian can be spared to go to France, where he will be Sir Geoffrey's second in command. Today he oversees a recruitment muster. Most of those who show up are locals, but a few are men who had heard Sir Geoffrey's call for experienced soldiers and have come to seek a place in his company.

Sir Brian is a veteran of such encounters and knows how to separate the wheat from the chaff. He looks for healthy, strong men, preferably with experience of war. If they have their own arms and armor, so much the better, but lack of equipment will not keep Sir Brian from choosing a likely soldier.

Some of the men, he knows, think only of the money—the archer's wage certainly, but especially the possibility of pillage. The customary pay rate for an archer is four pence a day, roughly what a skilled craftsman might earn. And as to the spoils of war—a successful expedition can make a man rich.

But trustworthiness is important. Sir Geoffrey's company will be small and each man will have to rely on every other. Thus Sir Brian looks most closely at the local men, whose characters he knows. But he must also balance the needs of Sir Geoffrey's military company with those of his lands. Life will go on at home when the soldiers travel to France, and it would not do to strip the manors of all the best men.

Sir Brian is careful to inspect all the equipment that is presented before him. The care with which it has been kept surely reflects the character of the man carrying it. Some of the men he knows, such as Gilbert Mercer, who has served well in the past. Others merit more scrutiny.

Still, some choices are easy. The tall stranger with the aketon and leather helmet has good experience. Sir Brian directs him to the clerk to have his name recorded on the roster.

"John Goddescalke," says the archer. "Called Long Jack, for good reason and true."

There always seems to be a project around the manor or village that needs the skills of Stephen Knoller the carpenter. This year he is working on the arbor to adjoin Lady Joan's herber. The arbor, like the village houses, is a timber structure built from substantial lengths of wood. The timbers are best grown in tended woodlands or chosen carefully from wild trees. They must be straight and strong.

But timbers must be worked before they can be part of a frame, and that is Stephen's particular skill. He has set a chosen tree trunk onto two heavy "horses," and has almost finished hewing the wood into a square shape with his side ax. He has preserved the heart wood in the timber's center for strength. When the trimming is done, he can begin cutting the joints that will allow this timber to be joined with others.

In addition to its agricultural resources, the manor has some manufacturing capabilities. Stephen Stout, the smith, makes basic goods in iron and occasionally steel. Here he discusses a possible flaw in a knife that he made for Thomas Stockbridge. Behind them is Stephen's forge, in front of which stands his great grinding wheel. Stephen holds little more land than his forge and house occupy, but he owes no agricultural labor. His work, for Sir Geoffrey or other manor folk, is paid work, and he earns more than enough to support his family and to pay his rents and fines.

Many of the various trades needed to keep society functioning were practiced in towns or on manors, but not all. Some craftsmen were itinerant, traveling from place to place as dictated by the demand for their trade or the availability of resources. A bodger, for instance, might set up his lathe in woods near a town or village. The fresh green wood of the forest was easier to shape than wood that had had time to dry out. Bodgers' many and varied products included spindles, bowls, tool handles, and shives and spiles (pierced bungs for casks, and their plugs).

Another itinerant craftsman was the thatcher, who constructed roofs of straw or reed. The seasonal availability of his materials dictated when he could ply his trade.

Sir Geoffrey's manor is compact, and most of its folk live in houses closely clustered around the manor house, but St. Mary's manor is more spread out. Some of those tenants and villeins live on lonely steadings, others in tiny villages. Their lives are more isolated, slower to respond to the forces that change the lives of folk more connected to the wider world. They are a conservative folk whose clothes, food, and furnishings are a generation or two out of fashion.

On this fine summer day, the wider world is coming to their doorstep.

Ralf, a villein's son, has spotted a stranger coming down the path from the forest. Like his elders he is normally wary of strangers, but he has spotted the pack on the man's back. He is a peddler, one of the itinerant merchants who bring manufactured goods to those who have no town or market close by. Ralf raises a shout to let everyone know.

Folk emerge from their houses and gather from the nearby steadings, eager to see what goods will be on offer.

The peddler unrolls a cloth, the better to display his wares. One by one he pulls them from his pack and sets them out for inspection. There are knives, fire strikers, and an ax, important tools for daily life. He has brooches, rings, and buckles of shiny pewter, cheap as such things go, but fine stuff for these poor folk. There are ribbons and hanks of thread dyed in bright colors, and the needles to use them. This peddler is a tinker as well, and his skill at repairing metalwork such as broken pots is also for sale.

Once the village folk have seen all there is to see, the haggling begins. Prices are not set in stone. Naturally the peddler wants as much as he can get. He would prefer to be paid in coin, but will trade in kind. The villages want to part with as little as possible, especially good coin.

Ports were vital landing places for the ships that carried foreign goods to England and English products abroad. Southampton was one of the most important ports in England.

England's most renowned export, fine quality wool, supplied a good part of the Italian cloth industry and nearly all of the industry in the Low Countries, and much of it left from Southampton. Other exports included grain, tin, and lead. Wine, mainly from Gascony, was by far the largest import for England, and Southampton was an important link in the trade with Bordeaux. Other common imports were spices, foodstuffs, fabrics, furs, dyes, mordants (dye fixatives), iron, copper, building stone, and forestry materials such as lumber and tar.

Trade with European merchants was vitally important to England. The crossing between England and Flanders or Gascony was short, and ships could arrive and depart year-round. But ships from Venice or Genoa made their long voyages in seasonal convoys. Luxury goods from the Mediterranean and the East, high in value and low in volume, were carried in galleys, sailing vessels that were also outfitted with oars. Cogs (oarless sailing ships), and the more modern carracks were used for less valuable bulk goods such as alum, a popular mordant that was in increasing demand for the developing English cloth industry.

Most goods were packed in barrels for transport, and merchants were obligated to return empty casks to their owners within an agreed upon time. It was up to the merchant to decide whether to carry the casks back intact (taking up valuable cargo space) or broken down (requiring him to pay for their reassembly).

Wine was generally transported in tuns (large casks of 400 to 500 gallons), though smaller-capacity casks were used for high-value wines and brandy. The volume of a tun was the standard unit for measuring the carrying capacity of a ship.

Ports were also a source of both royal and local tax revenues, from customs fees levied on export goods such as wool, fells, and hides, and on most imports. Taxes were assessed against foreign merchants and were usually calculated by the tun.

All this wealth could not move between ports unmolested. Ships were regularly menaced by pirates and by what would later be called privateers (captains holding a government's warrant to attack enemy shipping) and sometimes even by competitors from other ports in their own country. Southampton, like most ports, was vulnerable to attack. In 1338 the French sacked and looted the harbor and town, and among the many items lost was a substantial portion of the Crown's wine, which had been in storage there awaiting transport to London. As a result, King Edward III ordered that the town's fortifications be expanded and a militia formed. Even with the additional fortifications, it was decades before the Genoese trade through Southampton fully recovered. The war with France also made for hazardous travel between Gascony and England, and increased the cost of wine. The shipping fee for wine roughly doubled between 1337 and 1381.

In 1377, fears of a French invasion through ports in southern England were part of the impetus for King Richard's first poll tax. In Southampton, Sir John Arundel was put in charge of making extensive repairs to the fortifications, and the next year work began on a new keep.

Sir Geoffrey has business with Master le Fleming, and has taken a boat downriver to Southampton. He and his men would have preferred to ride, but Marjorie atte Well and Dionisia Lene are traveling with them on errands—Marjorie for Lady Joan and Dionisia for Ursula Doughty, who has taken over the Dunbury kitchen. Taking a boat down the river Test made the journey less of a trial for the women, and the women less of a trial for the men.

Travel by water within England is less common than by land, but boats can travel in weather that makes roads impassable. River travel can be quicker, especially when heading downstream. The rivers are important for merchants, as boats can carry more cargo than carts and run less risk of encountering brigands along the way.

Their boat lands just upstream of the town walls to avoid the crowded quay of the busy port. As they walk toward Bar Gate, Sir Geoffrey spies a leper begging beside one of the gates. Sir Geoffrey judges him to be truly in want, unlike many beggars who are simply landless men too lazy or thriftless to support themselves honestly, so he presents an opportunity to instruct young John Peel in the knightly virtue of charity. At a sign from the knight, Edward Manser, who carries Sir Geoffrey's purse, produces a coin for him to toss into the beggar's bowl.

 Many trades and crafts could only be full-time occupations in a town or city, where the potential clientele was large enough to support a craftsman. In some towns, craftsmen of a particular type might band together into a guild to control the practice of their craft and further their common interests, but this did not happen everywhere, nor for every craft. Towns, like markets, encouraged practitioners of a craft to group together in the same area. Thus, for example, the street of the goldsmiths was the place to find all manner of fine metalwork.

Cities and towns all over England supported a substantial business in prepared foods, because many town dwellers did not own cookware or lived in dwellings that lacked cooking fires. Cookshops offered ready-to-eat foods such as cooked vegetables, stews, and meats—fried, boiled, roast, or baked. Some shops took a customer's ingredients, enclosed them in pastry, and baked them for a small fee. Hucksters or regrators (small retailers, usually women) bought foodstuffs such as poultry, eggs, cheese, or fish for resale to individuals or cookshops, and were widely suspected of overcharging. Other vendors hawked fresh fruit or hot food in the streets, and their musical cries were a noted feature of town life.

Cordwainers made new shoes. They worked in suitable goat, deer, and calf leather which they bought from tanners (craftsmen who made animal hides into leather). The cordwainer cut the leather to a pattern, then sewed the inside-out leather together, shaped it on a last (wooden form), and added the sole. The fellow here is trimming excess leather from a seam before turning the finished shoe right side out.

Young John Peel is accustomed to the quiet routine of Dunbury manor, and is fascinated by the commotion inside the walls of Southampton. The long, busy thoroughfare called English Street runs the length of the town, over one-third of a mile from Bar Gate to Water Gate, and there are more people on this one street than in all of the manor. Everywhere he looks, people are buying and selling and hurrying about their business. Shops have wide windows open to the street, where craftsmen display their wares. Hucksters call out, extolling the merits of the foods they sell from baskets or trays. So many people, bustling from place to place, and all talking at once! There is so much to see—but he must spend the day listening to his uncle talk business. He begs to be allowed to explore the town instead. Sir Geoffrey has been expecting this and lets him go—subject to Edward's governance.

Painters decorated objects such as book pages, walls, statues, furniture, and banners, as well as creating paintings on wooden panels. Some practitioners were specialized: stainers decorated on cloth, limners created book illustrations, and painters worked on panels and walls. Like most medieval trades, painting was a male-dominated profession, but women plied the craft as well.

Here the painter repairs a damaged devotional diptych. On the chest behind her are her brushes of squirrel's or hog's hair and her colors, each in its own oyster shell. The pigments for her colors are mostly minerals, and the medium may be tempera or oil (usually linseed or walnut), depending on the pigment's requirements and the tradition in which she was trained.

At the table her apprentice is grinding an ocher pigment. He is also responsible for making the glue necessary for assembling the panels and the gesso used to prepare the surface for painting.

Girdlers made belts. Most often these were of leather, but they might also be made of woven stuff. Buckles were generally of pewter or copper alloy, and a strap end reinforcement of the same material was common. Often a girdler added metal mounts to decorate a belt. Belts fitted with buckles and mounts in precious metals were most commonly made by goldsmiths. This fellow is riveting a buckle to a belt.

Like young John Peel, Marjorie atte Well and Dionisia Lene are intent on making the most of the day. Marjorie is eager to visit her family and old friends, and Dionisia wants to do some shopping of her own. Once Marjorie has found Lady Joan's silk threads and Dionisia has placed Ursula's order for wine, they will be at liberty until they meet in the afternoon to return home. How quickly can they finish their errands?

With recruitment under way, and the growing likelihood that the king will not lead an army within the next year, Sir Geoffrey must apply himself to fulfilling his commitment to Sir John Stratton. His company will need to cross the channel to France, and he will require one or more ships to transport them. Such matters are not easily or quickly arranged. He turns to Gerrit le Flemyng for help.

Master le Flemyng is glad to have the opportunity to be of service. He has ordered his servants to prepare some refreshment while the men converse in the hall of his town house. Negotiations like these can go on for some time, and good food and drink will make the process smoother and more pleasurable.

Behind the men rise the carefully painted bricks marking out the fireplace's chimney. The chimney is constructed of real bricks, but they lie under a layer of smooth plaster painted with bricks, much more regular and visually pleasing than the real ones.

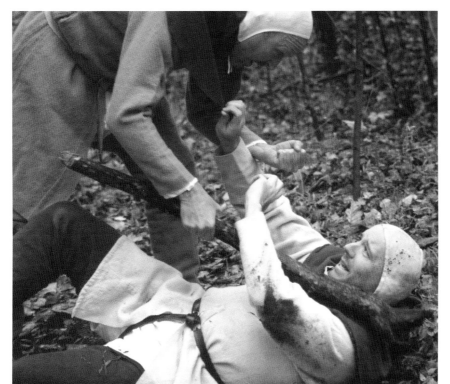

Back on the manor, the dispute between Thomas Stockbridge and John Arundel has taken an ugly turn. Thomas, having drunk a bit too heavily, has decided to beat some sense into John.

nglish archers are known across Europe for their skill with the sword and buckler.

A buckler is a shield so small that, if held close to the body like an old-fashioned knightly shield, it would be of little use. But a buckler is not used that way. Most often it is held close to the sword hand to protect it: even a slight cut on a hand or finger can render a man unable to hold his sword. Sometimes the buckler is held out toward the opponent, with the sword held safely back. This allows the buckler to stop an attack as it begins to develop. Whether sword and buckler are presented to the opponent, or buckler alone, the fencer's arms are usually held well away from his body, to keep his opponent at a safe distance and to keep his own, usually unarmored, body well away from the opponent's weapon. A buckler is not just for protection: once an opponent's weapon is safely controlled, the buckler makes an exceptional weapon for punching.

Stephen Stout claims that once, in a foreign land, he saw a book with pictures of men fighting with sword and buckler, showing many of the best fencing plays. Although Sir Geoffrey has been heard to say the same, most of the men do not believe it. Much of what the common soldier learns is by practice and from others who already have skill. It is the way that craftsmen learn their trades. What could be better?

As the long summer days roll by the crops are growing strong, and on some days the press of work eases. Long Jack, lacking any responsibilities, finds just about every day perfect for dozing.

Sir Geoffrey and the gentry men have been training to improve their chances of surviving a battle. Being a prudent captain, he wants his common soldiers to have a similar chance. This John Goddescalke is a resource that is going to waste with his slothful lounging. So Sir Geoffrey rousts the lazy fellow and sets him to work showing some of the manor men a bit of sword and buckler play.

Long Jack shows how easy it is to strike the novice Dobyn Taylor, who attempts to cut at his leg. Old Stephen Stout, a veteran himself, offers a correction to Long Jack's technique. Disdaining the advice, Long Jack presses on with his instruction.

Long Jack gets rougher, pummeling young Dobyn and abusing him with taunts. Thomas Stockbridge does not like the way this outsider is treating Dobyn, and says so. Long Jack agrees to let Dobyn off if Thomas will take his place. The match is short, as Long Jack quickly binds Thomas's sword against his own buckler. Jack's sword is free to thrust for Thomas's face and Thomas rocks his head back for fear that Jack will not stop his hand.

Gilbert Mercer has watched all of this and does not like what he is seeing. He is still hayward, it is still his duty to keep order, and this bully of a stranger bids fair to disrupt the peace. He must be put in his place.

Gilbert steps up to do just that. Briefly he holds his own in the fencing play, but this seems only to encourage Long Jack to push harder. In the end, Gilbert takes a hard blow.

Long Jack just grins.

The wheel of fortune turns as Stephen steps in. Long Jack soon finds he was wrong to dismiss the older man's skills, when Stephen deftly traps Jack's arms and gives him a well-deserved clout with his pommel.

AUTUMN

At summer's end, the grain is so heavy that the stalks are starting to bend. The orchards are bursting with fruit. It is nearly time for the harvest, and the laborers are hard at work in preparation. The sickles and scythes are sharp, the threshing floor has been cleared, and everyone is watching the weather for dry days.

Harvest time means the heaviest labor of the year. The grains must be reaped, their upper ends cut with a sickle, handful by handful, then bound into sheaves. Once the heads of the grains are cut, the rest of the stalk is mowed with a scythe, to provide straw for bedding, thatching, and other uses. Harvest involves all the men, women, and children of the manor, because it must be done swiftly so that as much of the ripe crop as possible can be gathered. The threat of rain at harvest time is a nightmare—in wet weather the crop may rot in the field. The specter of hunger is never far from a farmer's mind.

The lord's fields are reaped first and the manor folk gather for the task. Because they are working for the manor, Sir Geoffrey will provide their meal, with Marjorie atte Well and other servants bringing food straight from the manor kitchens. Before work they will get ale, cheese, and wheaten bread; at noon, more ale, cheese, and bread and a dish of fish or flesh; and when the day is done, another round of ale.

Once the grain is in, threshing can start. Threshing is the hot, hard work of beating the harvested grain stalks to knock the grain free of the plant. The men have stripped down to shirts and braes and rolled down their hosen to let the breeze cool them.

With the threshing done, the winnowing can begin. This process uses the wind to separate the heavier, useful grain from the lighter, less useful parts of the plant, the chaff. The grain is vital to people's food stocks and the chaff will be added to the horses' winter fodder.

All the work is overseen by manor officials, both to ensure that the tasks are done well and to prevent theft.

On the ancient mound of Dunbury near the manor, a fair has been held annually since time out of mind. Dunbury fair has declined from earlier days: Stockbridge has grown so large that its craftsmen and merchants can sell year-round, and the St. Giles fair at Winchester, several weeks before Dunbury's, draws away many dealers and their stock. Dunbury fair's patron, St. Mary's Nunnaminster, is not important enough to give it standing and promote it in the interest of increasing their own income. But it is still important to the countryside around Dunbury and the Wallops, because the vendors sell to individuals rather than trading merchant-to-merchant as they do at the great fairs. The days of the fair are days of holiday, entertainment, and profit, and when harvest duties permit, the local folk make the most of them.

The dealers set up shop in many kinds of temporary shelters, from large canvas-covered bentwood frames, to one-person folding booths, to rough lean-tos. Some do without shelter, selling from a roofless table or merely a stool. The least well-off sit on the ground or carry their goods with them as they move through the fair.

Entertainers, such as the juggler in the extravagant blue hood, will find their way to any fair, for the chance to work a crowd and perform for money. They add to the merriment and good spirits, but they also have a reputation for drunkenness and for inciting otherwise good folk to rowdiness and disreputable behavior.

John Arundel has found just the thing to bring home to Avis. His friends agree that it might sweeten her attitude toward his French adventure.

Robyn Taylor has a little coin to spend and wants to buy a fairing (souvenir) for Elisota Arundel. The girdler has many goods, and Elisota would look beautiful in this one. But it's one of the most elaborate girdles on offer, with all those fine pewter mounts. The girdler's wife sees his interest, but he quickly learns that he cannot haggle the price down far enough. It is far too rich for his purse. He will have to look somewhere else.

Traders offer a wide range of goods—agricultural produce such as corn and fells, craft products such as pottery and baskets, daily necessities such as cloth and clothing, and trinkets such as ribbons and cheap, shiny jewelry. Livestock and bulk food-stuffs are bought and sold as well.

Vendors wander through the crowd calling out for attention and touting the quality of their goods—a tray of hot meat pies, or a rack of savory pretzels. A waferer sits by her fire with her hot iron and bowl of batter, offering sweet, crisp waffle-like treats to any who have the coin.

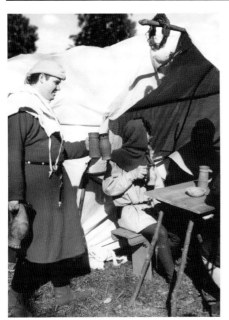

A popular attraction at the fair is the tavern, marked out by its traditional ale stake and vine wreath. The shaded booth with its table and benches offers a chance to sit for a few minutes and enjoy a refreshing mug of ale, or maybe even some mead (fermented honey beverage).

For discerning drinkers, this fair has a vendor with a stock of imported wines and brandies which he offers for sale by the glass. His prices are not cheap, but this is an opportunity for fairgoers to taste something out of the ordinary. He keeps the glass, of course, but he does wipe it off between customers.

Drinking at fairs can be a problem, and the preachers often rail against drunkenness and the bad behavior that comes with it. Sometimes a wandering friar will do so right in the middle of the fair, but not too near the tavern, lest he find himself being helped on his way by an unappreciative tavern keeper.

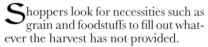

Shoppers look for necessities such as grain and foodstuffs to fill out whatever the harvest has not provided.

The jugglers, musicians, and puppet shows provide entertainment, but the fairgoers also make their own. In an open area, some of the men engage in a contest that would rejoice Robin Hood's heart: shooting at the popinjay. A "parrot" (a cloth body, stuffed and adorned with brightly dyed feathers) is set atop a tall post and the men take turns shooting at it, as they might at a lone bird in a tree. It takes a surprising amount of control to shoot almost straight up, and the possibilities for mocking opponents' failures are almost unlimited. To no one's surprise, in the end it is Hick Spryngot who brings down the popinjay.

Vendors coming to the fair must guess what goods will sell best and at what prices, and be prepared to haggle. There is always a risk of losing money, but the chance of making it is a powerful lure, one to which Sir Geoffrey himself is not immune. He has sent Geffrey Breton to sell the fells of sheep that have died or been culled through the summer and autumn. But a careful wife considers quality and price closely, and pays no more than she must.

Outside the tavern, Long Jack and some of the tenants have gotten up a game of knucklebones. It starts off peaceably enough, but they keep drinking while they play, and soon they grow rowdy. Good-humored abuse turns ugly when accusations of cheating erupt. First threats are exchanged, then blows, and the escalating brawl brings Stephen Knoller on the run, as he is serving as a beadle (peace keeper) for the fair. He is too late to save the tavern, which collapses as the fighters crash into it. It is the end of the fair for these troublemakers.

Early in September Sir Geoffrey's old friend Sir Robert de Charron, recently returned from Italy, visits the manor, and the knights take the opportunity for arms practice. Sir Geoffrey wears his old gambeson (padded under-armor garment), much besmirched by his haubergeon (mail shirt), and Sir Robert wears his traveling clothes. They start with the sword of war, a primary knightly weapon. Their swords are sharp, so their practice could be dangerous, but neither man is a novice at arms and both know how to withhold a blow, or soften it on the instant if harm might come to the other player.

While in Italy, Sir Robert met a soldier by the name of Fiore dei Liberi, a man of remarkable skill at arms who is making a name for himself as a master of fencing. He teaches a methodical and disciplined approach to combat. Sir Robert has learned some of Master Fiore's techniques and is eager to demonstrate them to his friend.

When swords cross in combat, a fencer must know what to do almost without thinking. His awareness of his opponent must be sharp, precise, and faultless so that he can act boldly and gain the advantage. As Sir Geoffrey tries to free his sword from the cross, Sir Robert feels the pressure leave his own sword; immediately he moves in and pushes Sir Geoffrey's sword pommel upwards. This controls the sword and opens Sir Geoffrey to attack. Were they wearing armor, this would expose the vulnerable armpit area to the point of Sir Robert's sword.

Master Fiore believes that all fencing is based on wrestling, and his techniques often rely on wrestling moves to finish the fight. The sword is often used to break the attack and open an opponent to a counter-attack. Sir Robert shows how, after deflecting Sir Geoffrey's attack, he can close and use the combined leverage of his sword and a leg behind Sir Geoffrey's knee to throw him to the ground.

Sir Robert demonstrates how to bind up an opponent's hands before striking him. He has caught Sir Geoffrey's downward cut on his blade. Seizing the initiative, he steps under the blades. His closing step allows him to slip his hand over Sir Geoffrey's blade and between Sir Geoffrey's hands. Sir Robert's pressure between the hands traps the weapon as long as Sir Geoffrey maintains his grip on his sword. With Sir Geoffrey's sword effectively harmless, Sir Robert can bring his own sword around for an attack.

Sir Robert helps his friend up from the floor. Sir Geoffrey is impressed by how effective the technique is and has Sir Robert show it to him again.

After working with the long swords of war, the knights shift to daggers, because a knight must be prepared to fight with many weapons. Blows are direct and powerful, not slashes: they must be able to penetrate heavy garments and even armor. Sir Robert steps aside from Sir Geoffrey's underhand thrust and uses his free hand to turn Sir Geoffrey, again setting up an attack.

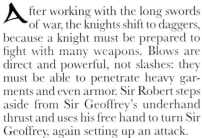

Then the knights move to the shorter side swords. As he did when they were using daggers, Sir Robert catches Sir Geoffrey's wrist as he strikes. A twist hurts Sir Geoffrey's elbow, forcing him out of position. Sir Robert can now hit his friend with the pommel of his sword or strike with the blade.

With an elbow push, Sir Robert gets Sir Geoffrey turned around, then stamps on his leg. He only knocks his friend down, but in battle such an attack, cleanly struck, can break the leg.

Sir Geoffrey demonstrates his own ability to use some of Master Fiore's techniques. He has parried Sir Robert's sword and forced it low, stepping in and putting a leg behind Sir Robert's. With an arm across Sir Robert's throat, Sir Geoffrey shifts forward, striking Sir Robert with his body to knock him off balance and throw him to the ground. It is a technique that Sir Robert used on Sir Geoffrey when the men fought with their daggers.

More plays follow until, hot and sweaty, Sir Geoffrey calls a halt. It has been a useful practice. Both men have gotten exercise, and Sir Geoffrey has learned some new techniques that will serve him well in combat.

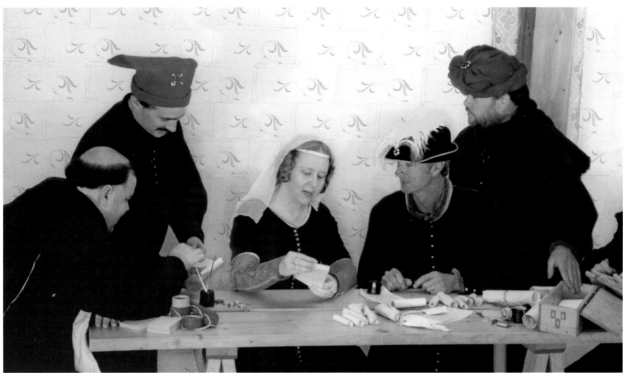

ichaelmas (September 29, the Feast of St. Michael the
Archangel) marks the official end of harvest and the
fiscal year. Contracts expire, debts come due, and Sir Geoffrey
holds a manor court to settle outstanding cases. The manor tenants are required to attend. They will pay their rents, fees, and
any fines levied upon them for transgressions, formalize manor
business, and celebrate the end of harvest.

The business of the day begins in the great hall of the manor.
Lady Joan acts as the *contrarotulator* (controller) for all of the Peel
holdings, auditing and counter-signing all accounts. Before the
start of court, Lady Joan and Sir Brian du Bois meet with the
stewards and bailiffs of Dunbury and the outlying manors to
review the year's accounts. Each must report in detail on rents
and fees received, expenses paid out, the size of the flocks, and
the amount of grain and other crops produced. Omissions or
inaccuracies must be made good by the officers responsible.

This year Lady Joan is driving the clerks to special care: the
manors must be in good order and their records up to date before
Sir Geoffrey's departure. Father Paul and Father Alan exchange
glances and prepare for a wearing day.

he clerks work through the
accounts from the outlying
manors, recording errors and
questions, and beginning to con-
solidate the separate reports. The
rough data is recorded on wax
tablets to be verified and eventually transferred to the permanent
account rolls.

The manor tenants come to settle the rents, fees, and fines incurred since the last court. The first occurrence of the Death killed many tenants, and the recurrences have slowed recovery. Sir Geoffrey's grandfather had to lease most of the demesne lands, which makes the Peels much more dependent on cash rentals than the yield of their lands. Sir Geoffrey is rigorous about collecting all that he is due, and this causes some disgruntlement among the tenants. In other parts of the country tenants have resisted or even revolted against demanding landlords—though never so spectacularly as this past summer—so the Peels must be careful not to overstep what is considered traditional.

Among the fines and fees to be paid are land rents, heriot (on the death of a tenant), merchet (for marriage of a child), and chevage (for permission to live away from the manor). Fines for breaking the customs of the manor will also be assessed.

There is a great deal of business to get through today. Before court begins, Sir Geoffrey confers with Lady Joan and the officers, reviewing what must be dealt with and the order of procedure.

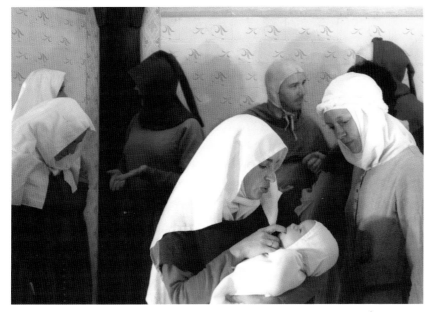

At the back of the hall, the tenants gather and socialize, waiting their turn to pay fines or appear in court, or simply watching the fun. Marjorie atte Well stops by to admire Isolda, Elena Spryngot's youngest child.

James Warde calls the hall to order, and Sir Geoffrey sits under his cloth of estate. Lady Peel and John Everard stand beside him, ready to assist with information. Young John Peel and Edward Upham are in attendance as well—their responsibility is to observe and learn, and they know that Sir Geoffrey will quiz them afterward. The clerks arrange their papers and turn to blank pages in their wax tablets.

The court opens with a check on attendance. Stephen Knoller asks that his neighbor Hick Spryngot be excused attendance, because he is sick in bed. Then the important matters of the condition of the manor are dealt with. Among the fines handed out is one to Stephen Knoller. He must pay three pence for cutting down an oak tree in Fishpondwood without leave of the lord or woodward.

Outstanding inquiries are reviewed. Gilbert Mercer, previously charged with inquiring into the circumstances of

Philip Doughty's death, reports that to all appearances, the cook slipped crossing the stream and struck his head on a rock. No one in manor or village had a quarrel with him, or reason to wish him harm. Sir Geoffrey finds that Philip died his rightful death and this will be reported to the king's coroner.

Manor officials who hold annual appointments, such as the hayward and woodward, are renewed or replaced.

Since Gilbert will be part of Sir Geoffrey's departing military company to France, he must be replaced as hayward. The tenants have elected Stephen Stout, Gilbert's predecessor, to replace him. Stephen swears the oath and Sir Geoffrey presents him with a wand of office.

Finally matters against the customs of the manor are dealt with. Among these matters is the continuing argument between Thomas Stockbridge and John Arundel over trespass by pigs. Sir Geoffrey calls them into court. Their strife has disrupted the manor and, as both are to go with him to France, he will not have them carry it along when the company leaves. He informs them that their differences are now settled and fines both of them.

Sir Geoffrey closes the court and retires to the chamber with Lady Joan.

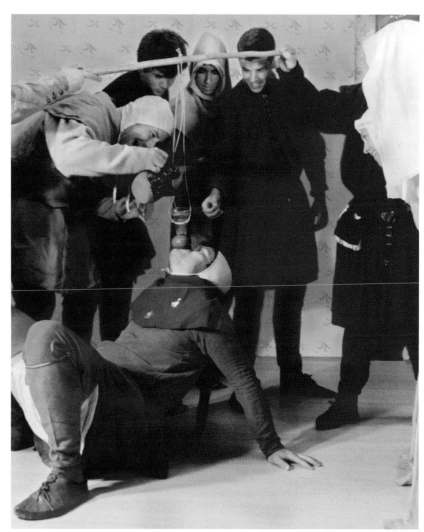

arvest done and court finished, it is time to celebrate. While the tenants wait for the celebratory feast to begin, they disperse to various amusements. Long Jack is still not especially popular, but he is a more than willing competitor in the drinking game that James Warde starts up at the back of the hall. John Peel is certain that those who wager against Jack will lose their stake, and lays his bets accordingly. To Jack he shows a penny, which he will add to Jack's winnings.

Some of the tenants escape out of doors, where the weather is fine and fair. A few of the men and boys start up a game of foot ball. It will be quite rough and tumble before they are through. Some of the younger lads get up impromptu races and wrestling matches. The children—and some of the adults—play a noisy game of hoodman blind, till in the rough horseplay one of the hoodmen is pushed and bloodies her nose on the stones of the well. Stephen Wallis pulls out his brother's old bagpipe and plays. Men and women gather, take hands and dance a carol that will soon be winding all about the village. Geffrey Breton's dog leaves his post with the hoggaster flock and joins in the fun, barking and racing about the dancers.

WINTER

Although most of the harvest is in and much of the threshing is finished, there is still a great deal of work to be done on the manor. The straw must still be brought in from the fields. Then the fields must be plowed and the winter crop—mostly wheat and barley—sown. This allows the crop to germinate before harsh weather sets in, giving it a head start on its growing season next spring and summer. Threshing and winnowing of the autumn harvest will continue indoors when poor weather makes outdoor work impractical.

In October, ripened fruits such as apples and grapes are gathered. Hick Spryngot's son Nicholas knocks the low apples from the tree so that they can be brought in for storage. Nestled in a bed of hay, the apples will give the storeroom a sweet, pleasant scent. Wild nuts, and fruits such as berries, hips (the fruits of wild roses), haws (hawthorn fruits), and wild apples also are gathered.

Wat Spooner, one of Sir Geoffrey's tenants, prepares to lead the manor's pigs out to the nearby woods to fatten on the forest's bounty. Wat carries a stick so that he can knock down any acorns that have not fallen. They will enrich the mast on the forest floor, a mix of fallen acorns, beechnuts, bark, roots, and fungi—fine fodder for a pig. The pigs will be set free to roam in the woods for a month or so, until time for slaughter. Tenants can pay to put their own pigs in Sir Geoffrey's woods, or to let them feed in his stubble fields.

No other animal is so easy to raise or so soon ready for slaughter as a pig. They are important to the tenants of the manor, as they provide a very economical source of meat. They need nothing but food scraps, except in the hardest months of winter. They can forage for themselves (though sometimes in someone else's fields) and they grow fat quickly on meager feed.

The only pigs to survive the winter will be the sows that have been bred and the best of the breeding hogs. Slaughtered pigs are butchered, salted, and dried to provide meat through the winter. Sausages and blood puddings are seasonal treats made from the blood, fat, and soft organs. The animals are also a source for lard and tallow, substances with many uses. A new foot ball is made from a pig's bladder, more fun with a few dried peas or beans tossed into it to make it rattle.

Elisota Arundel is harvesting teasels, the flower-heads of a variety of thistle covered with tiny hook-shaped prickles. Dried and mounted in a wooden frame, the heads will create a stiff, brush-like surface. Elisota and her mother use it to comb the wool that they will spin. Professional shearers (cloth finishers) use the same tool to raise the nap of woolen fabrics.

Avis Arundel carries a sack of grain to Sir Geoffrey's mill for grinding. The miller keeps one-twentieth of the grain as his multure (fee), and Avis will receive the rest back as flour and carry it home for baking. She will watch him closely, as millers are notorious for keeping more than their due.

Baking and brewing continue all through the year: grain and yeast, made into bread and ale, form the basis of the country diet. Some of the tenants bring their dough and other foods to the communal oven for baking. Newly refurbished, it still has raw earth on top and sides, but the villagers will soon cover it with turf to hold the insulating earth in place.

The Spryngots have funds enough to have a separate building behind their house for baking and brewing. Elena kneads wheaten dough into loaves and bakes them in her own oven, its stones heated for several hours by a fire built inside. After the ashes and unburned wood are raked out, the stones retain enough heat to cook several batches of bread or other goods. Atop the oven, next to a bowl of rising dough, she has placed a ceramic pipkin containing a remnant of unbaked dough; she will conserve it carefully, so that its yeast can provide the leavening for her next bread-baking.

The little building also helps Elena to provide additional income to the family; she brews ale to sell to her neighbors. She first malts barley by moistening it and allowing it to sprout. She toasts the malted barley, stirs together a mash of toasted grain and water, and sets it aside to ferment. Any ale that she sells is subject to testing by the aletaster, Stephen Knoller, to determine its quality and whether the price she charges is appropriate. Stephen is quite strict about violations, and although Elena is fairly careful about her quality and pricing, she was fined at the last manor court for overcharging. This happens to her and most of the other alewives in the village several times a year.

Winter is also the time for harvesting honey and wax. Honey is the primary sweetener—sugar is prized but too expensive for most people, or even for routine use at the manor. Honey is also used in medicines, and to preserve fruits so that they can be put on Sir Geoffrey's table throughout the year. Beeswax has many uses, including waterproofing cloth, treating bowstrings, filling writing tablets, sealing containers, making ointment, and providing the material for high-quality candles.

South of Dunbury in the New Forest, some folk keep bees in live trees; but Sir Geoffrey and his tenants use skeps, made from coiled ropes of straw. Alan Stone, one of St. Mary's villeins, is bringing an empty skep to the apiary; he will select the heaviest of the active skeps and drive the bees into the new skep. In early winter the bees are lethargic, less resistant than usual to leaving the hive. The process is simple, but needs skill and speed: Alan will invert the old skep and hold the new one above it so that their rims touch at a single point, then tap on the old skep until the drowsy bees crawl up into the new one. The new skep will replace the old in the apiary, and Alan will be able to remove the honey and comb intact from the old skep. He will keep the emptied skep for next summer, when he will attempt to attract a new swarm into it, and the process will begin again.

November is the time for culling the herds. The livestock have been getting extra feed, fattening them for slaughter. Winter fodder is limited and only vital animals can be spared—milk cows, draft beasts, and breeding stock. This cow is not among them.

Thomas Stockbridge holds the cow while Gilbert Mercer strikes it on the brow with the back of an ax to stun it. Then the men will cut its throat and drain the carcass. Almost all of the animal will be put to use. The blood and meat will become food, some to be eaten now, most preserved for the winter to come. The horns are of use to a horner for making into things such as combs and panes for lanterns. The hooves can be turned into glue, useful in many trades. The hide can go to a tanner, to be turned into leather. Even the bones have uses, carved into tools, toys, and accessories.

As November turns to December, the days grow shorter and the nights longer and colder. On the rare occasions when the clouds roll back, the sun rides low on the horizon. Travel becomes more difficult, communication with the outside world grows rarer, and the life of the manor turns inward. Though the work does not end, boredom is widespread, because there is less variety in each day.

With much of the winter's food stored away, the manor folk look toward laying in another vital supply: firewood. The common folk are not free to simply go out into the woods and cut down trees, since the trees are Sir Geoffrey's property. They must content themselves with dead wood gleaned from the forest floor, and what wood they can knock down by hook or crook.

To add to the family income, Avis Arundel has made an arrangement with a merchant in Stockbridge. He brings wool to her house, where she and the children wash it, card it, and prepare it for spinning. When the wool is ready, the merchant returns and collects most of the wool to distribute it to other workers for spinning. Avis keeps some herself and spins it; she can sell it to the merchant for a higher price than the unspun wool.

Although most women are heavily involved in turning raw wool into thread, and some weave for their families' use or for sale, most commercial weaving is done by men. Many kinds of looms are in use and they can be significantly more complex than the basic vertical loom that Avis uses. Horizontal looms with treadles, and broad vertical looms, allow production of cloth more quickly and in greater widths than is feasible on a home loom.

Elisota has placed her distaff in a stand to spin her portion of the prepared wool. The shaft of her spindle is wooden and the whorl is leaden. Avis saw a spinning wheel on offer at the fair, and though she longed for it, the price was too high. She consoles herself with the thought that, while the great wheels make spinning thread much quicker, they are not portable. She and Elisota, moving about the toft as they do their chores, would be unable to take their spinning with them if it were set up on such a wheel.

While Elisota spins, Avis weaves cloth on a simple vertical loom. As Avis works, the finished cloth is rolled onto the bottom and fresh warp (lengthwise threads) is rolled from the top. Items that Avis needs periodically, such as shears and balls of weft yarn (to be woven through the warp), are kept nearby.

Textile work goes on year-round, at all levels of society, and at the manor Lady Joan and her women are also hard at work, as they are almost every day. Today, however, they have turned to more delicate and decorative projects. Brightly-dyed silken cloths and threads helps to bring a little more color into the utilitarian objects of daily life, and gives the women the pleasure of making something beautiful.

Dame Katherine is embroidering roses on silk backed with linen. This is only the sixth, and she has nearly eighty more to go. When they are all complete, they will be cut out and appliquéed to a new bed (that is, bed hangings and coverlet). She is working in a technique known as *opus anglicanum* (English work), which uses primarily split stitch and couching. The silk-and-linen ground stuff is held to the frame with heavy hempen thread, and the tension can be adjusted by spreading the thread over the frame.

Lady Joan examines Rose Wilkin's latest attempt at tablet weaving, a technique for making very strong stuff good for belts, garters, trim, or other applications requiring narrow-ware. The warp threads are passed through holes in small squares of boxwood; as these tablets are turned different threads are brought to the surface to make the pattern, then the weft thread is passed through the shed (the open area between the raised surface threads and the rest of the warp) and pressed into place with an ivory beater to tighten the threads, and the tablets are turned again. The warp threads are attached to the uprights of the frame, enabling the weaver to maintain the right amount of tension on the warp threads and keep the shed conveniently placed. This very simple design uses heavy silk threads in three colors: white, orange (dyed with madder) and light green (dyed with weld and woad).

Marjorie atte Well is using lighter-weight silk thread to braid a cord that can be used for drawstrings, lacing, or decorative braid. This technique uses loops of thread in different numbers and a variety of patterns to create cords with profiles that can be flat, round, square, or even split. Some patterns are so complex that they require as many as three people and produce intricate raised designs. A single person's ability to control tension on the lace is restricted by her reach, so the length of cord that one person can produce is limited.

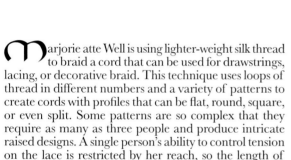

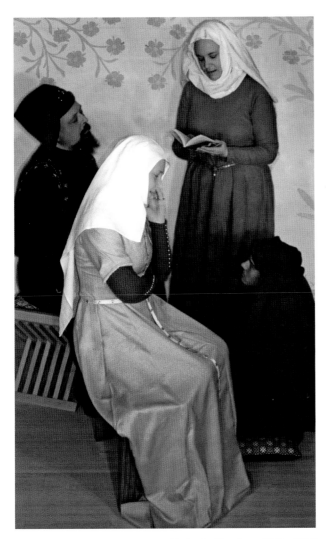

As the year wanes and the days draw in, the gentry turn toward indoor amusements.

On quiet evenings when only family is present, they may sit in the parlor and talk, or take turns reading aloud from one of Lady Joan's prized romances. She developed a taste for them while she was in service to the Countess, and over the years she has collected several books. No matter how many times they hear the stories, the Peels never tire of the travails of King Horn, the love of Floris and Blancheflor, or the adventures of Gawain.

Letters and travelers break the tedium with news and gossip. The king's intended bride is nearing the end of her journey to England. Lady Anne of Bohemia is the daughter of the emperor and the sister of Wenzel, king of the Romans and ruler of Bohemia. The king's council hopes that the alliance will shift imperial support toward England from France; Pope Urban worked hard to bring it about, in the expectation that it would strengthen support for his papacy. The wedding is scheduled for January, and great plans are reported. The parliament has been adjourned in the midst of debating new taxes so that the lords can get ready for the wedding festivities, now just weeks away. There is to be a tournament and Sir Geoffrey plans to attend.

Sir Geoffrey is more concerned about the politics of the marriage, but Lady Joan and Dame Katherine wonder about the two principals. The young king is handsome and cultured; his dealings with the rebels in the summer showed that he is brave and resourceful. Lady Anne is only a little older than the king, and gossip reports that she is a learned, devout, and sweet-natured lady—which probably means that she is not beautiful.

Nor does she bring much to the marriage, as Sir Geoffrey continually remarks; not only is there no dowry, but King Richard has committed to lending thousands of pounds to the Bohemians. And Wenzel's good will is no guarantee that his father, the emperor, will turn away from his French alliances. Worse, the Empire might try to use the marriage treaty to draw England into wasteful military adventures against the false pope in Avignon. Sir Geoffrey regrets the failed marriage negotiations with the Visconti in Milan—that match would have enriched the kingdom's coffers.

Chess and merels (nine-men's morris) are popular board games, but whenever William Cressy visits, he and Dame Katherine renew their enduring rivalry at tables. The pieces are among Katherine's most prized possessions: finely carved ivory with representations of monsters, heroes, and astrological signs.

Others seek outdoor pastimes, despite the chill. Sir Brian du Bois takes a few early-morning hours for one of his favorite pastimes—who knows if there is good fishing in France? With his carefully selected and prepared rod of willow, braided horsehair line, and lures skillfully made from bits of feather, he stalks the fine, fat trout of the Test. It is not an efficient way to catch fish for the table, but he is not troubled by that. Better, he believes, to be out and about than to sit cooped up in a house.

Charles Carpenter is a craftsman in the employ of Gerrit le Flemyng. He started the day feeling fine, but now is not well at all. Master le Flemyng notices and summons Alice Coventre.

Dame Alice is the widow of a physician. She helped him in his practice and learned much at his side, but she was not able to make a living in the art after his death. Few people are willing to trust a woman as a physician, and most of those who did expected to pay her less than they had paid her husband. Debt has forced her to take a position as a servant in the le Flemyng household, where Master Gerrit frequently makes use of her specialized skills.

Dame Alice sits Charles down in the hall of the le Flemyng town house and examines him, a process of great interest to two of the household boys.

As she questions him about his morning's activity, she observes his general condition. After taking his pulse, she fetches a glass uroscopy flask and has him fill it. Holding the flask against the light, she compares the color of his urine to painted pictures in the small folding medical handbook that was her husband's constant companion.

Dame Alice diagnoses an ephemeral fever, one of the many diseases caused by disordered bodily humors, in this case brought on by eating hot food on an empty stomach. Consulting her almanac, she checks the phase of the moon and the positions of the planets to verify that the day and hour are safe and appropriate for a suitable treatment: phlebotomy (bloodletting).

To those such as barber surgeons who were not trained physicians, phlebotomy was one of several possible treatments used to draw off an oversupply of bad humors. Less drastic treatments such as cautery (burning the flesh, for example with a hot iron) and cupping (placing heated cups over small cuts in the patient's skin) served much the same purpose.

Herbal medicines were also a large part of common medical practice. A practitioner might, like Dame Alice, have a manual with recipes for medicines, but would most often rely on memory, concocting medicines and applying them as he or she had been taught.

Practitioners like Dame Alice also cared for simple wounds with cautery or ointments, and treated fractures and dislocations. Here she has gotten two of Sir Geoffrey's archers to help her with a dislocated shoulder that the unlucky Charles suffered while loading supplies for Sir Geoffrey's expedition to France.

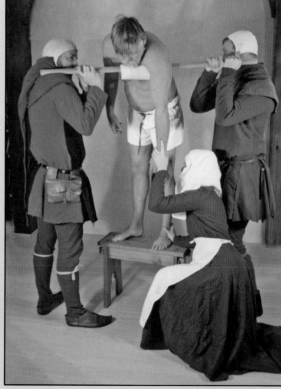

Doctors were rare in England throughout the middle ages. Treatment by a university-trained physician was the most desirable course, but physicians were not the only medical practitioners. There were also barber-surgeons, apothecaries, and midwives treating patients for a variety of conditions. Most large cities licensed and regulated medical practitioners, virtually all of whom were men. In rural areas, however, women also practiced medicine and surgery.

Medieval medical treatment was based on classical ideas about disease and the body. These ideas, codified by the revered Greek physician Galen in the third century, were transmitted to the West both through the Byzantine empire and, in Arabic translations, through Muslim Spain. The central doctrine of this system was the belief that sickness was caused by an imbalance in the four bodily humors, each of which had two qualities: blood was hot and wet, phlegm was cold and wet, yellow bile (or choler) was hot and dry, and black bile (or melancholy) was cold and dry. Medical therapies were intended to correct imbalances in the humors. A patient with a cough caused by phlegm would be treated with hot, dry medicines such as ginger or licorice, and "good wine well warmed."

Many medical practitioners owned recipe books or manuals that recommended standard preparations for specific diseases, to be formulated into pills, syrups, and medicated salves. Most medicines were herbal, and many included imported spices such as pepper, cinnamon, ginger, and saffron, as well as sugar or honey, all of which were sold by apothecaries. Other ingredients included locally available herbs such as borage, wormwood, horehound, violets, and roses. Olive oil, lard, tallow, and wax were used as bases for ointments. Opium—one of the few truly effective drugs in the medieval pharmacopoeia—was used in many medicines.

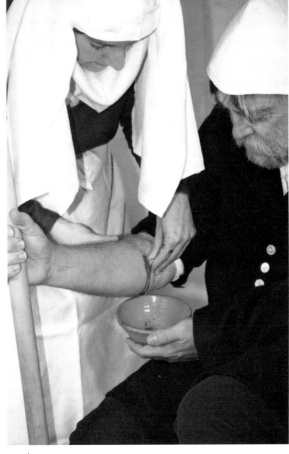

Dame Alice gathers her tools for the bleeding. She has a stout stick for Charles to grasp, a sharp knife for cutting, a bowl to catch the blood, and bandages to dress the wound when she is done.

Charles grips the staff tightly, making it easy for Dame Alice to find the cephalic vein. She makes a small slit, then squeezes the vein to control the flow of blood. Only a few ounces need to be taken, and all goes well.

She also prescribes a humor-balancing medicine: a cooling electuary (medicine in honey or syrup). As no rose sugar is to hand, she uses sandalwood, gum arabic, cloves, and musk to prepare *diarodon*, which she makes up into small lozenges.

Some of the letters reaching winter-isolated Dunbury bring news that may affect Sir Geoffrey's plans.

It is rumored that the situation in Flanders is growing worse, as the count of Flanders seeks to impose his control on the independent-minded burghers whose trade is so important to England. Some folk speculate that the king may go to war with the count to protect English interests. If so, Sir Geoffrey will answer the king's call to arms after all. He is troubled to think that he might not be able to help out his old friend Sir John Stratton, who was indeed named constable of Bordeaux in the autumn. And since the parliament has cut the war subsidies for the Aquitaine, Sir John will surely be hard pressed in his efforts against French incursions. Even if the war with Flanders does not materialize, can Sir Geoffrey really afford this expedition to France, where pay will likely be late in coming, if it comes at all?

Sir Geoffrey needs more information. How bad is the situation in the Aquitaine? How badly does Sir John need his help? As soon as Mass and breakfast are done, he summons Father Paul. It is time to write some letters of his own. High on his list is a request to the king's chancery for a letter of protection, as a precaution against unexpected legal proceedings while he is away. With such a letter in hand, his mind will rest easier at leaving his holdings in the hands of Lady Joan and his officials.

Father Paul has set up a writing station in preparation for handling Sir Geoffrey's correspondence. A wooden slope provides a slanted surface that makes writing easier, as well as offering places to hold two inkhorns and a pair of quill pens.

As Sir Geoffrey dictates his letters, the priest takes notes on a set of waxed tablets. He will read back what Sir Geoffrey has said and, if the knight has a better thought for phrasing, he can make changes easily by rubbing the wax smooth with his stylus's blunt end, and writing the corrected text. This process will go on until Sir Geoffrey is satisfied that the letter is as he wants it.

When Sir Geoffrey goes off to attend to other business, Father Paul sets his spectacles on his nose and writes out fair copies of all the letters, and a second copy of each to keep as a record. He carefully checks both originals and copies, corrects any mistakes, and seals and directs the letters.

He sends for a pair of grooms. To the first he gives the letter addressed to Sir John Stratton, instructing the man to carry it to Master le Flemyng in Southampton and inform the merchant that Sir Geoffrey wishes it on its way to Bordeaux as soon as possible. It may take days or weeks to reach Sir John, so it must leave at once. To the second he gives the letter to the chancery and a small purse of coin to cover the expenses the man will incur while carrying the letter to London.

After sending the most urgent messages on their way, Father Paul sits back to consider how best Sir Geoffrey's other letters should be sent.

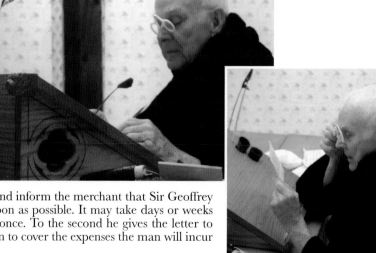

Sir Geoffrey, Lady Joan, and young John greet Lady Peel in the hall. She has come to stay at the manor through the Christmas celebrations and to evaluate the progress of her grandson's education. He seems to be coming along well, greeting her with a man's respect added to the affection of his childhood. She can see that he has grown impressively since she last saw him; his constant training has been good for him. This should be a pleasant visit, as long as she and Lady Joan can stay on good terms.

The kitchen is busy tonight; the staff has always been fond of Lady Peel, and this is Ursula's first opportunity to show her old mistress how well she has taken command. It is still close enough to harvest that there are no shortages of key foodstuffs, although the menu must accommodate the fasts and abstentions of Advent (the season of preparation for Christmas).

Like many knights, Sir Geoffrey hosts guests at dinner most days—an assortment of friends, relatives, travelers, messengers, and business associates. Since both his mother and William Cressy are visiting, today's meal is more elaborate than usual, but nothing like the feast of last Twelfth Night. In the less formal atmosphere, the food is simpler, and the wine is served in honest pewter rather than in expensive and fragile glass.

This makes a good opportunity for young John Peel to practice his service at table, under the close scrutiny of his watchful grandmother.

The conversation turns to the coming year. William has had word from London that Sir John Stratton still expects Sir Geoffrey in the spring. This news, traveling by friends of friends, has "crossed in the mail" with the letter that Sir Geoffrey dictated earlier in the day. Tomorrow the men will have to meet with Sir Brian du Bois to advance the plans for the expedition.

But tonight not all of the conversation concerns business. There is much talk of the king's imminent wedding and the associated festivities as everyone enjoys a fine dessert of crisp wafers and pears poached in wine. Gossip has followed Lady Anne of Bohemia's travels since she left Germany in late September, through Brussels, Ghent, Bruges, and Gravelines to Calais. She is said to have landed at Dover and to be en route to Leeds Castle, where she will spend Christmas.

Although the day has been short, it has been busy, and the Peels retire gratefully to their chamber. Marjorie atte Well and Edward Manser help them to undress, don their nightcaps, and climb into bed. Edward sets the urinal by the bed for his master's convenience, then draws the curtains against drafts ...

... and Marjorie blows out the lamp.

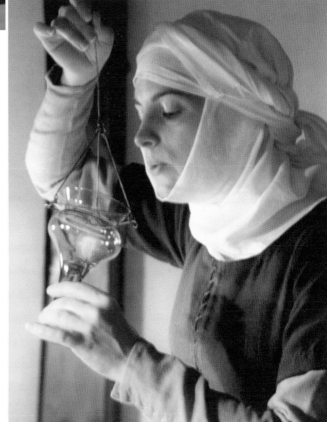

On Campaign
and
At War

On Campaign

The English armies of the Hundred Years War are no longer the feudal hosts of the earlier Middle Ages. When he goes to war, the king can no longer draw upon military obligations down the social hierarchy, from his great lords through their vassals to the lower ranks. Instead he offers indentures (contracts) to experienced captains and great nobles, who provide an agreed number of men for an agreed payment. To make sure that they can raise the men they have promised, indentured captains might subcontract further, as Sir John Stratton has offered to do with Sir Geoffrey. In this way they can call on suitable soldiers without having to maintain them.

Beyond daily pay, an important draw is the prospect of glory, spoils, and wealth obtained at the enemy's expense. The possibility helps the captains to retain soldiers in the ranks, often keeping commoners soldiering on even when they have not been paid.

By Sir Geoffrey's time, most of England's armies are made up of men who are essentially professional soldiers, men who make their living from war. However, they are not standing armies. Men come and go, organizations are fluid, and armies are dismissed when their immediate purposes are finished. Garrison units and the mercenary bands that shift from master to master are the only full-time soldiers.

To raise a large army for an offensive campaign, the king must call on men who have been living quietly as landowners, servants, artisans, and farmers since the last campaign. A hired army may include mercenary bands, but it is not simply a mercenary force. Most of the soldiers share ties of kinship, social obligation, and long acquaintance.

The English armies are unusually disciplined by the standards of the day, and they are almost entirely volunteer armies, selected from those willing to serve.

Sir Geoffrey's agreement with Sir John Stratton stipulates that he provide ten men-at-arms and twenty archers. Sir Geoffrey himself is one of the men-at-arms. Some of the rest are his higher servants and relatives, and others have been recruited from neighbors or from foreign soldiers currently without employment. Many of the archers come from among Sir Geoffrey's tenants and servants, some have been recruited from his neighbors' tenants, and—like the men-at-arms—some are full-time soldiers come into the knight's employ.

There are others who will travel with the company as well: servants for the gentry, cart drivers, a craftsman or two to maintain equipment, women, and even children. Many of the archers, especially the married professional soldiers, will not travel without their families.

Military strength is often measured in lances, what the French call *glaives*. The number and kinds of soldiers making up a lance have changed over time. At times it has included only the man-at-arms, and at other times it has counted his supporting troops, sometimes even his servants.

A man-at-arms may be a knight, a squire, or even a commoner who has acquired the necessary equipment. What matters is that he be armored completely, from head to foot, and be able to provide and equip his own horse so that he can serve as a cavalryman. Expert riding skill is not necessary. Indeed, the French chivalry (knightly class) ridicule the horsemanship of their English counterparts.

Yet social rank is still important. A knight's pay is twice that of a squire: two shillings per day versus one. A simple (commoner) man-at-arms can expect to receive the same pay as a squire, but he can also count on facing a struggle should he ever be placed in command of his betters.

Sir Geoffrey's lance comprises a man-at-arms, a varlet (manservant), and two mounted archers. Sir Geoffrey is the man-at-arms; the varlet may or may not be expected to arm himself and fight, and the archers will dismount to fight. Since the start of the war, the balance between men-at-arms and other troops has been shifting, both within a lance and in the army as a whole. In the last generation, a ratio of only one archer per man-at-arms was common in indentured retinues, but the proportion of archers has grown over the years. Sir Geoffrey has observed the change in the conduct of the war, and has readily adopted the newer model. With the war going poorly, fewer men of his class are interested in going over the water to fight in France, and even squires

are harder to find. But archers are still available, and cheaper than men-at-arms.

The young varlet holds Sir Geoffrey's banner, which displays his personal arms ("six pieces gules and Or, three bells Or"). The lad is on his first campaign and has been brought primarily as a servant. He will help Sir Geoffrey to arm, maintain his equipment, and attend to duties about the camp. The horse he rides is the knight's and is loaded with some of his equipment. The lad also leads a sumpter horse laden with more of Sir Geoffrey's baggage, and extra equipment such as the two lances snugged under the baggage.

The archers finishing out the lance are Sir Geoffrey's liveried men. They are much less expensive to hire than a knight. A mounted archer could expect to be paid six to eight pence, and an ordinary archer on foot three to six pence. Rates are lower for service in England than for service abroad.

As is common nowadays among retinues like Sir Geoffrey's, the archers of the company are all mounted, the better to travel swiftly. Although a mounted archer can expect a higher rate of pay, that extra pay must cover the expenses of the horse. Since some of Sir Geoffrey's archers have been horsed at his expense—at least initially—his clerks will deduct from the archers' pay to cover the costs of the animals and their upkeep. The men will not see any more money as mounted archers than they would as foot archers.

The archers carry all of their own goods, equipment, and supplies. Lucky or resourceful men might find space on one of the baggage carts for some gear, but they cannot count on it. Much more important things go on the carts, such as Sir Geoffrey's tent and barrel after barrel of extra arrows.

A wealthy knight should have several horses: the courser he rides into battle, a palfrey to ride on the march (to keep the courser fresh for battle), lesser horses for his servants, and a sumpter horse for his baggage.

A generation ago, a knight would have been expected to own a destrier, a heavy war horse specially bred to carry a man-at-arms in battle, as well as another horse to ride to and from the battlefield. This practice has fallen out of use, in part because English knights prefer to fight on foot and do not want the expense of owning and maintaining a destrier. Instead, Sir Geoffrey maintains a courser, a sturdy, strong, and nimble animal. While trained for the rigors of war, it does not have the finely honed fighting skills of a destrier.

His squire rides a palfrey, as Sir Geoffrey does when not in his armor. The archers ride whatever sort of animal they have acquired or had provided to them. This is usually an animal of no particular quality, such as a small hobby.

Sir Geoffrey Peel serves as the company's commander as well as one of its men-at-arms.

Sir Geoffrey's armor is quite complete. Plate armor covers his head, torso, arms, legs, hands, and feet. An aventail of mail hangs from his visored helmet and he wears a shirt of mail beneath his breastplate. This mail protects his elbows and armpits as well as giving him a little extra protection where his body armor ends and his leg armor begins.

Over his armor he wears a coat fringed and trimmed with silk and gold. Besides being fashionable, it helps to make the armor a little more comfortable by keeping it from the sun and wind.

Sir Geoffrey's armor is decorated with latten (an alloy of copper, usually brass) at the edges of several pieces. In some places, this is engraved

with prayers for protection, such as the one on his gauntlets: "*Mater dei memento mei*" (Mother of God remember me), and in others with merely decorative patterns. This adornment serves more than one end. Not only do the prayers make the armor more defensive and the decoration make it more handsome, but its presence helps to announce that Sir Geoffrey is a man of means—well able to pay a ransom, and therefore more valuable captured than killed.

Around his waist Sir Geoffrey wears his military girdle, a sign of his status as a *milites* (soldier), much as the ancient Roman soldiers wore their *cingulum* (military belt). Sir Geoffrey's belt is mounted with plaques that carry his coat of arms, proclaiming his identity as well as his wealth. His belt end (hidden, along with the buckle, behind his left hip) also has a prayer on it.

Sir Geoffrey's guidon is the flag under which his company will march. It has the red cross of St. George at the hoist, declaring the company to be English. The rest of the flag is in his livery colors of murray and azure (mulberry red and sky blue) and bears the image of his badge, a bell. Sir Geoffrey's banner (previous page) is displayed when the knight himself is present.

Gilbert Mercer serves Sir Geoffrey as his vintenar, the captain of his vintaine (twenty-man unit) of archers.

Gilbert is the most heavily armored of the archers. He wears a mail shirt and over that a simple breastplate. He has a mail coif for his head and shoulders, supplemented with a bevor (lower-face guard) that straps on over the coif. He tops it all off with a bascinet-style helmet. An old and successful campaigner, Gilbert owns all of this equipment. Unlike most of the archers, Gilbert owns his own horse as well, so he keeps the extra tuppence per day.

Les Gens d'Armes, or the Men-at-Arms, of the Company

Sir Brian du Bois has served Sir Geoffrey since he was a squire. His armor is nearly as complete and modern as Sir Geoffrey's, although he prefers the Italian fashion of wearing a mail shirt whose sleeve hangs over his arm harness. This is more flexible but less protective than the spaulders (shoulder guards) that Sir Geoffrey and William Cressy wear.

In one respect Sir Brian, an avid horseman, has a harness more up to date than Sir Geoffrey's. There is a lance rest attached to his breastplate. The curved arm can be folded down to help support a lance when mounted, and folded up out of the way when fighting on foot.

The squire William Cressy has taken an indenture with Sir Geoffrey to provide a lance of one man-at-arms and two archers. William himself serves as the man-at-arms on this campaign, but if he is called upon in the future, after he inherits his father's properties, he may send another man in his stead.

His body armor is of the type called "plates" or a "pair of plates," made of overlapping steel plates riveted to a leather covering. This is a fairly sophisticated piece of harness: tailored to the body, with large rigid plates to spread impact over the ribcage, and narrow movable lames over the abdomen. Like that of the other men-at-arms, his body armor is rounded over the breast, which helps to deflect weapons and arrows. And since the armor does not lie against his torso, a blow that makes a dent might not reach his body, and a blow that penetrates the armor might not draw blood.

Not all of the men-at-arms are of gentle birth like John Peel (far left), but most are men of at least some wealth, since complete armor, equipment, and a horse are expensive.

James Warde and his son David are commoners. Their equipment is not as finely made and fitted, nor as extensive, as that of the richer men-at-arms. David's helmet lacks a visor. James's has one, though he has removed it, revealing the hinged pivots to which it attaches and the chain holding the hinge pin on the side of his helmet.

War can lead to wealth and status for a lucky common man. The famous Sir John Hawkwood is said to be the son of a tanner, and he has earned rich lands in Italy.

John Langton is a squire indentured to Sir Geoffrey. Like William Cressy, he provides a lance to the company, although he has allowed Sir Geoffrey to choose the archers and only pays for them. He also serves as Sir Geoffrey's marshal, which makes him responsible for the company's horses. He sees to it that they all are well fed, watered, and shod, and in good health. He also ensures sufficient fodder and arranges for any replacement

horses that become necessary. He does not do the physical work himself, of course, except for some exercising of the animals—which he finds no work at all.

Sir Hugh Hulgrave is not one of Sir Geoffrey's regular associates. He has taken service for the duration of the contract with Sir John Stratton.

The fine fabric of his arming coat shows that Sir Hugh is a man of wealth, well worth ransoming.

His helmet, though, has a visor of an older style. It is essentially flat, lacking the snout that is now the fashion. Sir Hugh is an old campaigner, accustomed to his helmet as it is, and sees to no reason to change what works well for him.

Johann Hennequin, a lad recommended to Sir Geoffrey by Martin, is on his first campaign. Sir Geoffrey has accepted Johann despite his inexperience, trusting his old comrade Martin's assurance that the boy will be worthy.

Johann's helmet is his father's, and a little large for him. Like Martin's it has a *klapvisor*. Johann has removed the visor, revealing the attachment points and the rotating pin that will lock the visor to the helmet.

Martin Alemand is a little down on his luck, having been captured in his last battle and subjected to a high ransom. Martin was glad to hear that Sir Geoffrey was looking for good men. He has traveled from his home in Hamburg, in the Empire, to serve under his old campaign companion.

Martin's captor kept his armor, so he has had to equip himself with an older harness belonging to his family. Though old-fashioned, the harness still meets the requirement that a man-at-arms be armored at all points (completely).

As is common in his country, he wears a bascinet with a *klapvisor*, a center-hung visor.

The plates that protect his arms are each pointed to his gambeson by leather thongs through the mail sleeve. Each piece must be tied on individually, since the arm harness is not a single assembly as in more modern armors.

The sword is the weapon most closely associated with knights; yet swords are used by other soldiers, and knights use other weapons.

Swords come in many varieties.

Sir Brian du Bois holds a fine example of a side sword, the sort of weapon a knight might wear at his belt. It weighs less than three pounds and has a tapered blade which, among other things, makes it quick and handy to use. This sword is about equally good at cutting and thrusting and is designed to be used one-handed.

A falchion is a wide-bladed sword designed for heavy, chopping blows. It can strike powerfully but is harder to control than more classically formed blades.

For battle, knights favor the longer swords of war. These swords have hilts long enough for a second hand to grip them, yet they are light enough that a man can swing one with a single hand. They rarely weigh more than four pounds.

A sword of war can be used to deliver powerful cuts, devastating to a man in little or no armor. But they are of less use against the increasingly popular plate armor, being unable to cut through the metal. Men-at-arms, however, have developed techniques to use such swords against other men in armor. Most of these techniques rely on thrusting the point into weak spots in an opponent's harness. For greater effect, a fencer can grip the blade itself to improve his control of the point, stiffen the blade to thrust more effectively, and allow him to apply greater power.

In this clash of armored men and swords of war, the knight in blue has taken advantage of his opponent's eagerness to press in closely. He is reaching out to control his opponent's elbow and will soon have him turned about and vulnerable.

Other weapons are in use as well. Many are specialized to crack, crush, or dent armor. Though English knights rarely fight mounted, they do make use of their lances, usually by cutting them down to a more convenient length for use as spears, an effective weapon for thrusting into the weak points of armor.

One weapon of particular virtue against plate armor is the poll ax. Sir Geoffrey's poll ax weighs about six pounds and is a little longer than he is tall. Earlier axes were shorter, and later axes will be longer.

The ax blade can be used to make powerful cuts that can dent, and possibly cut through, plate armor. It will certainly wreak havoc on a lightly armored man. On the back of the head is a spike, which a well-placed stroke can certainly drive through plate. The long spike on the head of the ax and a corresponding one at the other end (the queue) can be thrust into the weak points of a harness. It is a versatile weapon requiring both hands to use.

In combat, the queue can be used for fencing until its wielder gains an advantage. Here Sir Geoffrey has caught his opponent's awl spike just behind the head. He uses his superior leverage to force the awl spike down, then steps in quickly as he thrusts his queue past the other man's head. Sir Geoffrey's opponent may think that he has avoided the knight's attack, but Sir Geoffrey's next move is to use the shaft of the ax (and a well placed knee) to topple the other man to the ground.

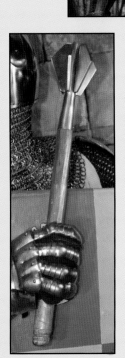

A mace has a heavy metal head on the end of a shaft. It is a powerful crushing weapon and a good blow from it is hard to withstand. Unlike a sword, where the weight is balanced close to the hand wielding it, most of a mace's three-plus-pound weight is well away from the hand. This makes it awkward to change the direction of a blow once started. Yet the blow is almost certain to be effective no matter how it lands, because crushed and deformed armor can hamper movement or effectively cripple the wearer. The mace is a weapon of power, not finesse.

The war hammer is a descendant of the mace. Like the mace, it is a weight-forward, awkward weapon. Unlike the mace, it has been specifically designed for use against plate armor. To achieve this, the design forces the wielder to be more discriminating in how he strikes. Either the hammer end or the spike end must hit cleanly in order to be effective.

Archers are the most common English troop type during the war, to the point that during the middle part of the war muster rolls usually list only two types of troops: men-at-arms and archers.

At the beginning of the war, almost all archers were foot soldiers, but as *chevauchées* have come to dominate English strategy, archers have come increasingly to be mounted. They still fight on foot, but horses give them strategic mobility. Towards the end of the war, as strategies evolve, mounted archers will decline in prominence.

Though the term "archer" can be applied to any soldier with a missile weapon, English archers are renowned specifically for their command of the war bow, also known as the English bow or, from about the middle of the fifteenth century, the longbow. The length of a war bow is supposed to equal the archer's height plus a handspan. It is made of a single stave of wood, and each end is capped with horn to protect the ends of the wood from wear. The smooth surface of the horn nock also reduces wear on the bow string.

Arrows are about a yard in length. Goose feathers are the most common fletching materials. They are split, cut to shape, and glued to the shaft, then the ends are tied down; sometimes a spiral wrap of thread is used to reinforce the glue, which might loosen in wet conditions. The nock end of the shaft is reinforced with a sliver of horn to take the shock of the arrow's release from the bow.

Like so many things, arrowheads have changed during the course of the war. Long-pointed heads of mild iron, called bodkins, seem to have been common at the start. About the middle of the fourteenth century another type became popular. They are similar to modern broadheads except that the tines are swept back toward the shaft. These new arrowheads are heat treated to harden the point.

The archer at left is typical of archers at the beginning of the war. He has no armor at all and wears the clothes he had on his back when he arrived at the mustering point. Like many of his fellows, he has a dagger at his belt, but unlike some he has a sword as well.

For the Prince of Wales's 1355 campaign, men from Cheshire and North Wales were issued white and green cloth from which to make tunics and hoods. This is one of the earliest approximations of a uniform for English troops. As early as Edward I's Welsh wars of the late thirteenth century, some soldiers wore the red cross of St. George as an emblem of allegiance, and that marking became a standard English field sign. The French used the white cross of St. Denis.

Archers will remain a major part of the English army throughout the war. While their clothing and armor will evolve according to the fashion of the time, their renown will remain unchanged. This fellow, from the end of the war, wears no armor, relying on the multiple layers of his doublet. He wears a helmet with a movable visor, in a common style called a sallet. Some archers of this time wore breastplates or brigandines (body armors of small plates riveted into a cloth garment), sometimes over a short-sleeved shirt of mail.

The Archers of the Compagnie

Long Jack Goddescalke (in the red hood) wears a helmet of hardened leather. Though not as effective as a steel helmet, or even an iron one, it will resist a sword cut and is far lighter. He has wrapped the liripipe (long tail) of his hood around his head to provide padding.

For body armor Long Jack wears his aketon of padded and quilted cloth, stout enough to resist cuts and to soften blows.

Hick Spryngot (in the brown hood) has a bascinet-style helmet with a padded lining sewn into it. It has been provided by Sir Geoffrey from his stocks of arms and armor and is a little large for Hick.

Hick wears no body armor. He finds it interferes with the drawing of his bow. He does, however, wear Sir Geoffrey's livery as he is the knight's sworn man.

Thomas Stockbridge wears a helmet that he has acquired on his own. It is not well made, but it is of metal. Steel scales are riveted in two rows to a leather band which is in turn riveted to the solid rings that make up the helmet's cap. Like Long Jack, he wears a badge on his hood depicting St. Edmund, the patron saint of archers.

Wat Spooner's helmet is also a poor man's helmet, even though it comes from Sir Geoffrey's stocks and is of metal. The two sides are riveted to a central band. This is a much simpler construction method than the sophisticated raising technique used in making Hick's bascinet.

John Arundel's helmet is like Wat's and, like Wat's, still shows the marks of the hammer blows that shaped it. He has used his livery cloth to cover a padded garment, armor he has made himself for his protection. John's sword is a family heirloom, said to have been carried by his great-grandfather when he served in the army of King Edward I. With its straight, flat cross and heavy, untapered blade, it is certainly not made for modern swordplay.

Stephen Knoller is a valuable man to have along. While he is not a master of the bowyer's craft, his knowledge of wood, learned as a carpenter, means that he can easily judge when a bow needs replacing, and at need can make one himself.

John Gregory is one of the professional soldiers Sir Geoffrey has recruited. He has padded body armor and his bascinet, while of riveted construction, is supplemented by a bevor and aventail, giving him far better protection than his companion, Richard Crispin, who has only a bascinet. In the back, wearing livery, stands Brian of Sherwode, a professional soldier who has served with Sir Geoffrey before.

Roger Forster and Daniel Dalroun are archers supplied by William Cressy as part of his sub-indenture to Sir Geoffrey.

Andrew Lange, Godfrey Kylly, and James Bailey are three more of Sir Geoffrey's liveried men. James is the best equipped, with padded body armor in Sir Geoffrey's livery colors and a bascinet with an aventail.

Edward Manser wears a *chapelle de fer* (iron hat). The broad brim protects him from downward cuts while the openness below the brim makes for easy breathing and good vision.

Thomas of Calais also wears a *chapelle de fer*, but it is of an older style and simpler construction—several plates connected by bands and riveted together. The broad brim means that he must take it off to shoot his bow.

Piers the Fletcher and Charles Carpenter are notable among Sir Geoffrey's archers as representing two generations: son and father.

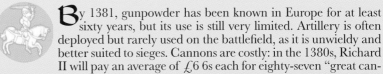

By 1381, gunpowder has been known in Europe for at least sixty years, but its use is still very limited. Artillery is often deployed but rarely used on the battlefield, as it is unwieldy and better suited to sieges. Cannons are costly: in the 1380s, Richard II will pay an average of £6 6s each for eighty-seven "great cannons of copper."

In addition, black powder itself is tremendously expensive. At a cost of eleven shillings per pound of powder (in addition to wages of sixpence per day for an ordinary gunner and one shilling per day for a master gunner), only the richest captains can afford to field firearms. The expense, and the difficulty of procuring powder, mean that there are generally few guns and a meager supply of powder. And since stone balls are the most common projectiles, there must always be stone carvers on hand to painstakingly cut and shape them.

Gunners are generally regarded as a class apart from other soldiers. First, there are some superstitious fears that the explosive powder might be the gift of the devil. But more important, it is dangerous to be a gunner: the unreliable devices often explode, killing those around the gun rather than those at whom the gun is aimed.

Although cannon and handguns play a minor role, they presage changes to come. While a fourteenth century gun is slower to load and fire, and less accurate, than a crossbow, it requires far less skill. And unlike the war bow, it does not demand a lifetime of practice.

Drew Bowden is a noteworthy member of Sir Geoffrey's company: a hand gunner. Despite his unusual weapon, he is counted among the archers.

At right, Drew loads his handgun. First he pours gunpowder into the gun's muzzle. Then, having dropped the ball into the muzzle, he tamps down the wadding, which will hold the charge and the shot in place. Finally, he primes the touch hole with more gunpowder.

Below, he has touched his burning slow match to the priming powder. The burning primer charge has ignited the main charge, which has explosively fired the shot out of the muzzle.

Some Other Troop Types of the hundred Years War

While English armies use the war bow almost exclusively, other peoples such as Germans and Italians prefer the crossbow. Genoese mercenary crossbowmen fought on the French side at Crécy. It takes long training and great strength to use the English war bow, but this is not true of the crossbow, and the heaviest versions can shoot further and hit harder than any war bow.

The crossbow, particularly the heaviest bows with more complicated spanning mechanisms such as cranks or windlasses, have a much lower rate of fire than the English bow, but the bow's advantage may be less decisive than it appears. An archer who shoots as quickly as he can will exhaust his arrows in a few minutes, and both archers and crossbowmen can use pavises (large shields of wooden planks) that protect them except at the moment of shooting.

Certainly when the Genoese crossbowmen at Crécy were thrown into battle while still exhausted from a long march and without their protective pavises, they suffered badly from the English archers. But in later battles, when English bowmen in Burgundian service will fight against Swiss crossbowmen, the English will show no obvious superiority.

Each of the crossbows above has a stirrup to aid in spanning the bow. The man in the foreground is bracing his bow by inserting his foot into the stirrup. After hooking the string with the spanning hook hanging from his strong leather belt, he will use the power of his leg muscles to span the crossbow, drawing the string back against the tension of the prod (bow) and settling it into a groove on the nut, a cylinder of ivory or bone set into the stock of the crossbow and connected to the trigger. Then he will draw a quarrel (bolt or arrow) from the case at his belt and lay it into the groove on the stock, seating it well against both the stock and the string. He will keep the quarrel in place with his thumb as he raises the crossbow to aim.

The man in the background rests the stock against his cheek, the better to aim. When he has found his target, he will close his fingers against the trigger. Inside the stock, the trigger mechanism will release the nut. The nut will revolve, the string will be set free, and the quarrel will spring forth.

The Genoese are famous throughout Europe for their crossbowmen. They are steady, well-trained professional soldiers, who serve in many armies and are especially popular as missile-armed troops in France.

Crossbowmen are often more heavily armored than bowmen. This man wears a mail shirt under a pair of plates. He has a bascinet helmet with an aventail of mail. The belt that supports his spanning hook also has a case for his quarrels, covered with water-repellent badger skin.

A hobelar is a lightly armed horseman, apparently named for his mount: a small, cheap, sturdy horse called a hobby. A hobelar is expected to have a helmet and some sort of body armor, and carries a light lance.

Troops of this type have been in English military service as far back as 1166, and they remained an important component during the early part of the Hundred Years War, filling functions that no army could do without: scouting, foraging, and pillaging. Many hobelars are of Irish origin, veterans of the brutal wars on the Scottish border. Hobelars are highly mobile, well suited to war fought in an open countryside and accustomed to fast-moving, destructive warfare. That, and the fact that they are relatively cheap, makes them a good fit for the English strategy of *chevauchée*. They will become less common as the war goes on, perhaps because mounted archers can fill the same role.

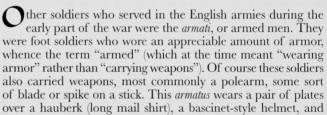

O ther soldiers who served in the English armies during the early part of the war were the *armati*, or armed men. They were foot soldiers who wore an appreciable amount of armor, whence the term "armed" (which at the time meant "wearing armor" rather than "carrying weapons"). Of course these soldiers also carried weapons, most commonly a polearm, some sort of blade or spike on a stick. This *armatus* wears a pair of plates over a hauberk (long mail shirt), a bascinet-style helmet, and plate leg harness. *Armati* rarely wore the leg harness of a man-at-arms, since such protection was expensive and difficult to march in.

Well-armored infantrymen of this sort were often seen in the better-equipped urban militias. At a minimum, a member of the London watch was expected to have a bascinet, gauntlets, and a shirt of mail.

Since Britain is an island, all travel between England and the continent is by sea. It is not always an easy journey because weather can prevent the ships from sailing when and where they want.

Southampton is one of England's major ports, and is often used to embark troops for France. Thus it is natural for Sir Geoffrey to take ship there for Bordeaux, where he will meet with Sir John Stratton and finalize plans.

At left, a small fleet of cogs sets out from Southampton. They are not naval ships, as England has no standing navy. Ordinary merchant ships are hired (or sometimes ordered to make themselves available) when the king wants them. Sir Geoffrey has made his own arrangements and, with Master le Flemyng's help, he has gotten a good price for his passage. While Sir Geoffrey does have a significant amount of baggage, it does not take all of these ships to carry it. Wisely, he has chosen to sail in convoy with other ships heading for the same or nearby destinations to reduce the danger of attack by hostile ships or pirates.

It is always important to know what lies in your path. Local people can be questioned, but they may lie. It is best to send reliable men of one's own to scout ahead of the army. Besides determining safe routes, they will spy out sources of supply, enabling the army to support itself by foraging from the countryside. Mounted men are best because of the speed at which they can travel, but horses can be noisy; men must sometimes dismount and creep about to remain unseen.

Being on campaign sooner or later means camping. Having a camp means that someone has to do the labor of setting it up, making it work, and taking it down again when it is time to move on. Given their station among the three estates, "those who work", the commoners are assigned this labor.

Several of the archers are setting up a pavilion for one of the gentle men-at-arms under Gilbert Mercer's guidance. Some of them have never dealt with a tent before, but Gilbert has a lot of experience. He knows what to do and how to do it quickly and with the least amount of work.

Besides getting the tents set up, the soldiers must build the gentry's fires so that their food can be prepared. Today John Gregory has drawn that duty. He has emplaced the uprights of the framework that will allow pots to be hung over the fire, and now concentrates on digging a suitable pit so that the fire will not ignite the grass.

Some of the archers, like John Arundel, share camp chores with a group of mates. John's cooking area is not nearly as grand as the gentry's, but it gets the job done. John is making a meal from foods that he has bought locally or obtained through forage.

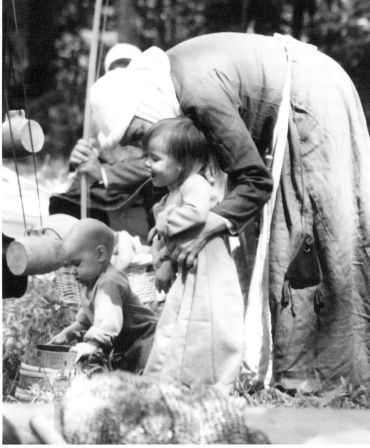

Campaign life is not just for men. Some of the archers have brought their families with them, rather than leave them at home with no one to provide for them. The wives do chores such as laundry and cooking, but they expect payment. There are also some unmarried women along. They will do chores, too, but sometimes they offer their favors as well, and competition among the men can be heated.

Sometimes the lands they travel through are not friendly to the English. They may be held by French sympathizers or by some lord with only his own interests in mind. Even with a safe conduct, there is always the possibility of trouble. Here John Arundel fills a collection of costrels (flasks) from a stream while Gilbert Mercer, bow ready, watches for any sign of unfriendly attention.

For the common soldier, a camp usually means sleeping under the stars with no more than a cloak or a blanket for a bed. It is an uncomfortable way to spend the night, but soldiers grow accustomed to it.

They expect to be in this camp for a while, so they have worked to make it more comfortable. Using wood they have gathered locally and the canvas covers from the company's wagons, they have cobbled together rough shelters.

A soldier's equipment requires continual attention. Hick Spryngot has found some shave grass and is using the tough reeds to scour rust from his buckler.

John Arundel works at cleaning his sword. It's a bigger job than it ought to be, because he did not clean it properly before sheathing it last time.

Stephen Knoller inspects the horn nock on the end of his bow. If the groove is too rough, it can dangerously abrade the bowstring.

Children, as children do, find things to play with. Here little Jak has discovered that the costrels, hanging from a cooking frame, swing and sway marvelously when he slaps at them.

The adults find time for play as well: some of the archers engage in a game with a stick and a ball.

More serious play starts when a pair (a set, usually three) of dice come out. In a time when playing cards are rare, various dice games are the gambling pastimes of choice. If actual dice are not available, the knuckle bones of an animal can be used; bets are placed on how they will come to rest after a toss.

On any campaign, there will be times when things get out of hand, times when order must be imposed. Discipline is important in a military company and the commander is its source. This dawn sees the swift application of justice as Long Jack stands once more before Sir Geoffrey for brawling in the camp. He is fined sixpence, which will be deducted from his pay. Behind Sir Geoffrey, John Arundel pays off a lost bet—he had been certain that Jack would get away with it again.

There are many rules for the conduct of troops on campaign and in battle. Sir Geoffrey has laid out thirty-four different regulations for his men to follow. Robbing a fellow soldier of his supplies, crying havoc (the signal for pillage to begin) without leave, raising a banner or pennon to lead men out of the army without license, burning without permission, despoiling territory that has surrendered, and breaking a royal safe-conduct are all punishable by death. Lesser punishments apply to lesser offenses.

Sir Geoffrey, too, is subject to rules prescribing how he may order his men and his campaign. Ransom may be demanded, but not an unreasonable one that would cause the prisoner to lose his estate. Commoners should be taken prisoner only if they assist the enemy. Children should not be held to ransom, nor the blind, the aged, or churchmen, as long as they have not meddled in the war.

There is often a wide gap between the codes and customs and soldiers' actual behavior. The laws of war seem to be kept best when they coincide with the men's self-interest. Since a captor one day might be a prisoner the next, the English and French men-at-arms tend to treat each other fairly well. The treatment of civilians is more variable and often brutal.

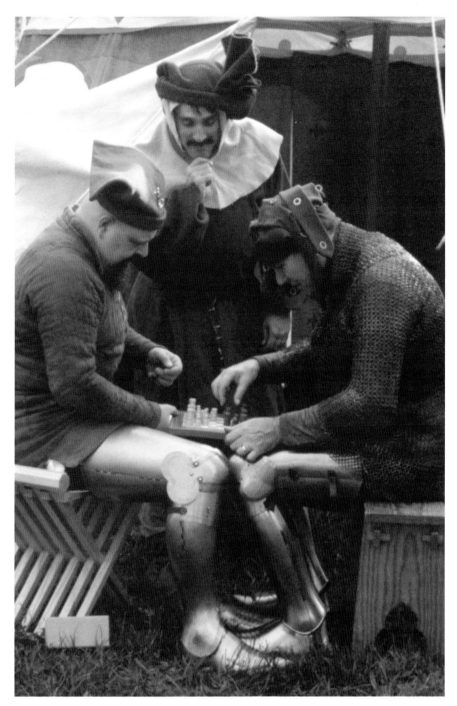

Sir Geoffrey, having servants and therefore free from caring for his own gear, would seem to have much more leisure time on his hands than the archers do, but appearances can be deceiving.

Running a military expedition is a serious business. Supplies are always a concern, as is the nature of the country around them: what it may yield in supplies, how it may be traveled, and whether it is safe. Sir Geoffrey does not simply rely on his scouts' reports but often wants to see things with his own eyes. He is the ultimate authority for dealing with anyone the company encounters, from a farmer seeking to sell them some food, to a band of *routiers*, to a local lord who may or may not be reliable. Successful negotiations are a vital step in making sure his company gets where it is headed.

When not so engaged, however, he and the other men-at-arms can participate in nearly all of the activities they might enjoy at home, except dalliance with the ladies. Here Sir Geoffrey and William Cressy are absorbed in a game of chess as James Warde looks on and offers advice.

Since the camp is in disputed lands, the men wear part of their armor to be better prepared should unexpected trouble arise. Leg harness is not too uncomfortable to wear, if attached to a well-fitted gambeson which distributes the weight, preventing strain upon the spine. But torso armor is another matter, and even arm harness will tire a man out. William, being younger—or perhaps more concerned—wears his haubergeon and standard (standing collar of mail).

If trouble appears suddenly, Sir Geoffrey will quickly wriggle into his mail shirt and slip on a helm and gauntlets. Though not full armor, it is certainly good protection, much better than the common soldiers are likely to have in a surprise attack.

Deeds of Arms

Deeds of arms (armed encounters) on foot or horseback are popular, not just among the men-at-arms who perform them, but also with those who watch.

Encounters on foot are better than mounted combat to reflect the skills needed in modern warfare, in which the English man-at-arms so often fights dismounted. One or more pairs of men-at-arms, or two equal groups, may consent to do combat under agreed conditions. In these times such deeds almost exclusively involve opponents from national enemies, such as Englishmen fighting against French or Scots, and take place either during a lull in a campaign or during a time of truce. Sharp weapons are used, but the rules and conventions of these combats, and the effectiveness of the armor worn, limit the risk.

For a single combat the pair normally agree to fight until one or the other has struck an agreed number of blows with each of the chosen weapons: for example, three with spear, three with sword, and finally three with ax.

These combats can be quite impromptu. In one case a French knight's offer of single combat was immediately accepted, although so late in the day that the English army took him along with them to do the combat the next day. On another occasion, a French knight traveling with an Englishman was so insistent on doing a deed of arms that the Englishman found himself jousting with sharp lances the next day, in armor borrowed from the Frenchman. At the other extreme, such a combat might involve weeks or months of negotiation, followed by travel to a prepared site in the marketplace of a major city or outside its walls.

In the fourteenth century the term "hastilude," rather than "tournament," is the catchall term to refer to a variety of martial games. To Sir Geoffrey's grandfather, a tournament was a mounted melée between two teams of armored men on horseback, all fighting simultaneously in a mock battle. By the late fourteenth century this particular form of contest has fallen out of favor. Such tournaments continue to be invoked in art and literature, but as a reference to an earlier age. When Sir Geoffrey attends a "tournament" he expects to see a jousting contest. When he attends a hastilude he expects to see a wider array of martial skills on display. The largest of these "hastiludes" are often international affairs for which men travel hundreds of miles, or even cross the English Channel to participate.

Jousting is a specific form of martial game. In the joust, pairs of armored horsemen armed with lances run (ride their horses) at each other. While each joust is an individual contest, the jousters are still divided into two teams, with each course consisting of a jouster from one side running against an opponent from the other. The tilt (barrier dividing the jousters) has not yet come into use. The danger of a collision between the horses remains a risk for both participants.

The most formal jousts share much of the pageantry of the old-style tournaments. Crests and armorial surcoats make a brave show, as jousting is both sport and theater. Often a team of jousters wears matching livery. During Edward III's reign, teams appeared at London jousts dressed as the Pope and his cardinals, and as the Seven Deadly Sins. At the first marriage of John of Lancaster, the king, his sons, and other nobles jousted disguised as London aldermen. In 1390 King Richard will head a team of twenty knights in matching livery, wearing his badge of a white hart, each led on a golden chain by a lady, all the ladies also wearing matching livery.

William Cressy, eager to display his prowess, has arranged to try the mettle of a French man-at-arms, Guichard d'Alès, a squire like himself. He waits now at the appointed place, armed and ready, attended by his man Daniel Dalroun and taking his ease in an arming pavilion. Daniel is the first to spot the approach of d'Alès and his party.

A quickly arranged combat might happen at a siege, or when two armies are near each other but not ready to offer battle, or when a man-at-arms is traveling under safe conduct in enemy territory and finds cause or opportunity to issue a challenge. William Cressy's combat has been arranged with the knowledge and permission of the local commanders on each side.

Neither William nor his counterpart is wealthy enough to employ his own herald, but each has arranged to use a herald employed (or borrowed) by his superior to take care of the necessary formalities.

Such combats are often designed to ensure that neither side has an advantage in equipment, as it is more honorable to defeat an opponent through your personal virtue than through superior weaponry. Thus William's herald offers d'Alès his choice of two similar swords.

’Alès requested that they begin their encounter with a *juste à pié*, a joust on foot, and William readily consented. Since neither has a visored helmet to hand, they agree to avoid strikes to the head, which could be lethal. The combatants approach each other at a good pace with their spears to their breasts.

They further try their skill, fencing with spears to test their mastery of the weapons, while still avoiding face strikes. When they complete these passes with the spears, they move on to an exchange of blows with swords.

encing with swords is not mere brutal and artless bashing. Above and at right, William conducts a deliberate and deceptive maneuver. First he reacts to an overhead blow from d’Alès by raising his sword as if to block it, while stepping to one side. William lets his own sword fall away upon contact. D’Alès, committed to his attack, cannot stop his slightly deflected sword as it travels toward the ground. Then William starts another step forward, turning to face d’Alès while bringing his own sword around, using the energy from the brief sword-on-sword contact to make the move faster and easier. William will strike as he completes his step, choosing any of the targets on the exposed d’Alès. Most are protected by armor, but if the fight were in earnest, William could direct his blow to d’Alès’s face as easily as to the gap exposed behind the flare of d’Alès’s gauntlet and his vambrace. Instead, William strikes his blade against the Frenchman’s chest just below the throat, as a sign of what might have been.

All is done under the watchful eyes of the heralds who, having discharged their duty as go-betweens, now serve as arbiters of the combat. Since the combat was so quickly arranged, the only other spectators are the servants the squires brought with them, who hardly matter. Both of the squires long for a larger, more noble audience, since unwitnessed deeds are little better than no deeds at all. They must content themselves with knowing that their borrowed heralds serve men of worth. While noble eyes will not view what they do this day, noble ears will hear of the day's deeds as the heralds spread the word of what has passed on this field.

William and D'Alès "touch" to indicate that combat is at an end. The normal restraints on violence are restored.

There is a real fellowship between opponents in such deeds of arms. When a man challenges someone to meet him in a combat, the formal language of the challenge speaks not of enemies or opponents, but of companions. In the conflict between their kings, each will do his best to see that his side prevails, but they share a common set of values, code of ethics, and sense of their chivalrous calling. Each understands the other in a way that someone outside their estate cannot.

The rich display of a formal deed of arms offers a pageantry that even the gentry do not experience every day. Add the excitement of the sport's inherent danger, and there are all the necessary ingredients for a popular entertainment.

The focus of a tournament is, of course, on the upper class—as hosts, participants, and spectators. But so rare and spectacular an event attracts people of all sorts. Servants and hired laborers in great numbers are needed for the work behind all the pomp and pageantry. Spectators are attracted by the color, noise, and excitement, and the crowds in turn draw vendors, entertainers, and malefactors hoping to use the occasion to their benefit. Sometimes fairs and festivals are held in conjunction with tournaments.

Jousters can build international reputations. The Flemish chronicler Jean Froissart celebrates the prowess not only of his countrymen, but also of English, German, Bohemian, and Castilian jousters. It is not uncommon for the announcement of a joust to include an offer of safe conduct so that foreign jousters can attend.

The great helm, no longer a common sight in battle, continues to be used in tournament, sometimes with an extra plate to reinforce the face plate. Other styles of helm specialized for the joust are starting to appear.

This great helm has a mantling of rich fabric surmounted by a red orle (thick ring of cloth) wrapped with gilded cord. The crest of molded and painted leather is a fanciful bat-winged horse, and peacock feathers sprout from its mane.

All that fine and expensive decoration is unlikely to survive the day.

At the fairs held alongside tournaments there is generally a bias toward goods of interest to the tournament participants, such as saddles and other horse paraphernalia. The tournament itself provides a chance to showcase the finest horses and interest potential buyers in them or their offspring.

The commoners present are at least as eager as the gentry for a show, but the mythological themes and fantastic trappings of the pageants presented to the nobles probably seem stilted and obscure. A singer of bawdy songs, an acrobatic mountebank, or a juggler of daggers is more to their taste. If they are lucky, someone might bring a bear for baiting: dogs are set on a captured bear, and the spectators wager on how long and how many dogs it will take to kill it.

At a large, public deed of arms, townsfolk and peasants crowd against the barrier fences, jostling for the best view. Such a close and rowdy crowd could impinge on the refined sensibilities of the ladies for whose honor and approval the jousters contend. Berfrois (elevated viewing stands) are erected so that the ladies may watch the contests. Some privileged commoners (in London, for example, the mayor and burgesses) are permitted to watch from a berfrois as well. Fine cloths are draped over the raw wood of the galleries to add to the festive ambience.

Between events, the fences and other equipment are kept in storage. In fact, taking charge of jousting paraphernalia was one of Geoffrey Chaucer's jobs during his term as the king's clerk of the works.

Musicians are an important part of the event. At the fictional tournament in Chaucer's Knight's Tale, the air rings with "trompes loude and clarioune."

Although Stephen Wallis is Sir Geoffrey's gentleman of the hall, he also plays the shawm and other instruments. Like most entertainers, he occasionally performs for other employers and sometimes for tips at a tourney, although he risks losing his salary if such a performance conflicts with pay day at Sir Geoffrey's hall. Here he and Julian join one of the Southampton waytes, hired for the day, to provide music for the Peels' viewing stand.

Sir Geoffrey has agreed to do combat with a French knight, Sir Guillaume d'Azincourt. The challenge was formal, with letters back and forth to negotiate the terms. A safe conduct was arranged for Sir Guillaume. The place and time were agreed and they have come to a prepared field, ready to essay combat before the assembled lords and ladies—and commoners—of the area.

Sir Geoffrey wears coat armor that displays his arms, and Sir Guillaume wears a jupon (sleeveless, fitted over-armor garment) of splendid fabric. Both men wear the armor they would wear for war.

They begin their combat on horseback. They ride three passes and Sir Geoffrey, though an indifferent horseman, manages not to embarrass himself. All the same, all three passes go to Sir Guillaume.

The knights continue on foot, first with swords. They clash blades, seeking advantage.

Sir Guillaume shifts his grip to his blade to prepare for a powerful thrust.

Sir Geoffrey, caught with his sword out of position, drops his blade and steps in to throw his opponent to the ground with one of the wrestling moves he learned from Sir Robert de Charron.

Sir Geoffrey is victorious in all three of the sword passes. The knights move on to the last phase of their combat: three passes with daggers. The first goes to Sir Geoffrey, the second to Sir Guillaume.

The knights begin their final pass. They circle each other cautiously, each watching for a misstep on the other's part. Thinking he sees an opening, Sir Geoffrey strikes with a downward thrust. It is a powerful blow, the sort that can pierce mail.

But Sir Guillaume has deceived him. The French knight, one hand on his dagger's hilt and the other on its blade, intercepts Sir Geoffrey's attack. It is a strong block, and stops the attack, but is only the first part of the French knight's ploy.

Stepping in, he shifts his arm over Sir Geoffrey's, trapping his dagger and dragging him off balance. With a quick pivot, Sir Guillaume hurls the English knight to the ground. The final pass goes to Sir Guillaume, who prevails in the encounter.

The Day of Battle

An English army in France is usually outnumbered. This is not surprising—France has a much larger population than England. More important, French troops are defending their homes, so the king and commanders can raise troops more easily. Most French troops are levies, ill-trained and ill-equipped men serving under feudal obligation, but many are men-at-arms. The French usually have a much higher proportion of men-at-arms than the English. Often the men-at-arms alone outnumber an entire English force.

An army is usually divided into *batailles*, or battles. On the march these are known as the Vanward, Mainward, and Rearward (front, main, and rear). On a battlefield, they may be referred to by number, as First, Second, and Third. Just as an English army is made up of men-at-arms and archers, so too are each of its battles. The French are more likely to organize a battle out of a single kind of soldier: all men-at-arms, or all crossbowmen.

Most of the English men-at-arms will dismount to fight on foot. Their horses will stay nearby, ready for either pursuit or escape. A small reserve of mounted men-at-arms may stand ready to exploit any favorable situation.

The terrible loss at Crécy in 1346 showed the French that mounted troops alone could not defeat determined soldiers and massed archery in a strong defensive position, but the notion galls the French knights, who consider themselves the finest chivalry in the world. Each new generation thinks that the knights of Crécy somehow failed as knights. These young gallants cannot believe in the strength of the English system until they experience it themselves. Yet since Crécy, wiser men have sought ways to defeat the English system. These attempts do not always work, but rarely is it because French courage fails.

The man-at-arms preparing for battle wears braes, hosen, and shoes as his inmost layer. He might wear a shirt, although some authorities recommend that he go without and have a satin lining for his gambeson instead. The gambeson is padded, to cushion blows and reduce chafing from his metal armor.

The arming process is intricate. William Cressy's man Daniel Dalroun prepares the harness to ensure that the process will go smoothly.

Once William has donned his gambeson, and it is laced to his satisfaction, they start putting on his metal armor, called collectively his harness. The harness is attached from the ground up. First his shoes are covered with flexible sabatons (foot armor of multiple plates), which are laced down at the toe to keep them from flipping up when he walks.

Next, carefully shaped greaves are put on his lower legs. Each is followed by a cuisse (to protect the thigh) with an attached poleyn (to protect the knee). Flexible lames (narrow strips) attach the poleyn to the cuisse and to a small plate below it which will be strapped over the greave, allowing the joint to bend. The top of the cuisse has a leather tab with eyelets. This provides a place for it to be pointed (laced) to the gambeson, much in the same way that ordinary hosen are attached.

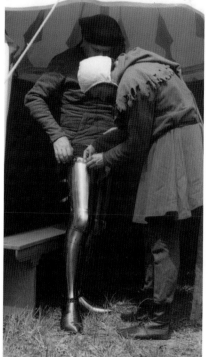

William's haubergeon is a neatly tailored shirt of mail providing flexible protection for the torso and arms. The neck hole of the haubergeon must be large enough for him to get his head through. Since this means that the mail will not cover his neck, he will also wear a close-fitting standard to protect his neck. The looser skirt of the standard lies over the haubergeon, covering any gap.

Over his haubergeon, William wears a pair of plates. It is composed of a single-piece breastplate and a clever arrangement of smaller, overlapping plates, all riveted beneath an outer covering, in William's case of leather. The armor buckles closed in the back.

He then dons his arm protection. This is an articulated piece for each arm, covering it from shoulder to wrist. The shoulder cap and the narrow lames between it and the upper arm are riveted to leather strips and allow considerable range of motion. The couter (elbow covering), like the poleyn, has a solid plate connected to the upper and lower pieces by lames and a projecting wing to help protect the inside of the joint.

Once arm, leg, and body armor are in place and William is satisfied that all is buckled and laced tightly in position, Daniel belts on the scabbard of the arming sword.

William's *chapelle de fer* is next. Daniel snugs the ties of the straps under his master's chin. Red and white plumes fit into a plume holder riveted to the helmet and lend a brave and jaunty air.

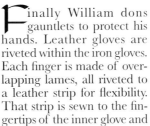

Finally William dons gauntlets to protect his hands. Leather gloves are riveted within the iron gloves. Each finger is made of overlapping lames, all riveted to a leather strip for flexibility. That strip is sewn to the fingertips of the inner glove and riveted to the solid plate that protects the back of his hand. This arrangement ensures that the protective metal stays in place over William's fingers.

Now fully armed, William Cressy is ready for battle.

On the day of battle, the archers prepare as well. Their armor comes in a wide variety of materials and has varying degrees of completeness. Unlike the men-at-arms, they have no servants to see to their arming. They must do for themselves or get a comrade to help, as Thomas Stockbridge helps Gilbert Mercer to strap on his breastplate.

Long Jack laces up his aketon. It has a padded, stand-up collar to guard his neck, and a heavily padded body which will stop most sword cuts; but the sleeves are only lightly padded, so that he can bend his arms and use either bow or sword. On the breast of the aketon he has sewn the cross of St. George, now much faded from wear.

Preparations continue. Bows are tested and strings checked for fraying. Arrow bags are stripped from their sheaves, the best arrows selected and tucked under belts so they will be close at hand.

When the horn calls for assembly, the archers march out of camp. Some of the women follow along, carrying water and a few extra arrow bags.

Protection from charging cavalry is vital. Sometimes the battlefield offers a natural feature such as a hedge, ditch, or swampy ground behind which the archers can stand. Even a simple slope helps, if the archers can be on the uphill side. When Nature does not provide, the archers must improvise. At Crécy and other battles, they dug pits before their lines. A horse that stepped into such a pit would fall, possibly breaking its leg. Nothing breaks the momentum of charging cavalry like having the lead horses in a charge go down.

Pointed stakes to protect the archers are well known from King Henry V's victory at Agincourt in 1415, yet that battle seems to be the first record of their use by an English army.

As the moment of combat comes closer, men's thoughts turn to their mortality. Many kneel and pray for their safety and for victory. Some bend down and take up a bit of earth to put under their tongue, a symbolic acknowledgment that they are dust and will return to dust. Perhaps such humility will make God look more kindly on them in the coming battle.

Archery, especially as practiced by the English, can be a powerful force on the battlefield. It can wound or kill both man and horse. It can sow disorder and destroy morale. But it has never won a battle by itself, and both sides know this.

The English man-at-arms, like his French counterpart, has firm faith in the protection of his armor. Only at close range is it likely that an English arrow or French crossbow bolt will penetrate. A man-at-arms expects to reach the enemy line.

Horses, not riders, are the preferred target for the English archers. Horses are larger targets than men. It is harder to armor them well, and it takes a very strong horse to carry the weight of both its own armor and an armored man. It is not necessary to kill horses, however, as a wounded horse can be more disruptive to a cavalry charge than a dead one.

Even if many horses are killed or wounded, French men-at-arms will almost surely reach the battle line, probably in strength. They must be met with men-at-arms, the troops with the best chance to stand against them. The English men-at-arms will be on foot, a steady, confident block of infantry. Their example serves to steady the archers as well.

The French may have learned that a mounted charge is no sure thing, but since mounted men-at-arms move much faster than those on foot, they suffer the arrow storm for a shorter time. Nowadays the French generally advance some men on foot and others mounted, trying different arrangements and timings in an effort to bring down the English.

Men-at-arms on foot begin their advance from beyond archery range, well over two hundred yards. This is a long way to walk in armor. Heads down as if pushing into a storm, they come on. Men without visors avert their faces. Those with shields raise them against the fall of arrows. Archery takes its toll as they advance.

However good the aim of the archers and however heavy the arrow storm, sooner or later the battle will come down to handstrokes, where the desperate struggles of individual men will decide the day.

Although English archers can, and often do, throw themselves into the fray, handstrokes are primarily the province of the men-at-arms. It is what they train for, and it is what they are armed for. It is where they will defeat the French men-at-arms.

Weapons of many kinds are in use, but with the increasing prevalence of plate armor, more and more men are relying on weapons that can be used for a solid thrust, such as the awl spike used by the knight at left. The awl spike is essentially a spear made only for thrusting, the most effective attack against an armored man. It has a rondel at the base of the spike, which acts as a stop-thrust as well as a guard that helps ward off opposing weapons.

The swords of war that have been in use for decades are changing too. Modern swords have stiffer blades with a more pronounced taper, designed to improve their thrusting capabilities. They can still be used powerfully to smite an opponent, but more and better plate armor makes such a blow less effective. The weak points in a harness, such as the armpit where only mail and the gambeson beneath protect a man, are vulnerable to a thrust. The enlarged modern grips, where a man can place both hands at once, permit a two-handed thrust—much more powerful than a single-handed one.

As armor has improved, soldiers have adapted. They have learned that gripping the blade enables them to make an even stronger thrust. Since a sword only cuts when the edge is drawn against flesh, gripping the blade is safe for the wielder as long as his hand holds steady. This grip improves control of the point and allows a man-at-arms to put his entire body's strength behind a thrust. A man-at-arms using this grip can also use other parts of his sword effectively against an opponent.

A blocked attack, accompanied by a quick step out and around, allows Sir Geoffrey to set his sword against his man's throat, ready to throw him to the ground if he does not yield.

Sir Geoffrey intercepts a thrust and diverts it. He will use his sword's crossguard to set it aside further.

Then he slams his sword's pommel up and under his opponent's visor, a blow that the Frenchman's aventail cannot stop.

Fighting in close quarters is normally the province of the men-at-arms, but once the battle lines have closed and there is no longer room for archery, or perhaps when there are no more arrows, even the archers come to handstrokes.

Lightly armored as they are, they must be cautious in engaging a man-at-arms. He is almost certainly better trained at arms than they are, but while his armor protects him, it does slow him down and often restricts his vision. Once a man-at-arms is isolated from his fellows, the archers can use their superior numbers and agility to gang up on him and tip the balance.

Raining blows from all directions, they can swamp his defenses. They can find the weak points in his armor, slip around behind him, trip him up, or tie up his weapon so that it is not free to swing at another archer. Like a pack of wolves attacking a bear, they can overcome him with their numbers.

When they do, they may kill him—the prudent course of action early in a battle when fresh enemies may soon come up. Archers are brutally practical men, and know that a dead man-at-arms is no threat to them.

But if the fighting is drawing to a close, another option presents itself. An outnumbered and outfought man-at-arms can be captured and held for ransom.

Ransom! A wealthy knight can pay enough to set a common man up for life, even after Sir Geoffrey takes his commander's share. Sometimes they do not even have to wait until the ransom is paid: Sir Geoffrey has in the past paid cash for a captive. It was not as much as the captors might have gotten if they had waited, but it was good coin—and in their hands.

Little wonder the men are elated by the day's good fortune.

To the victors go the spoils! It is perhaps the oldest rule of war. Sir Geoffrey's archers expect to be able to take whatever they can from the dead and the prisoners, from a defeated army's camp, and usually from a captured town.

Sir Geoffrey expects them to bring all that they take to a central location so that it can be valued and its worth shared out fairly among the company. Metal items are smashed and stamped flat so that they will pack tighter for transport. Strongboxes and chests must be brought before Sir Geoffrey before they are breached. Bolts of cloth, fine furnishings, and clothes are hauled to the growing pile. To be sure, a few looted items disappear into personal bags or are secreted away for later, private recovery. Sir Geoffrey knows this, and he will punish any soldier who is caught at it.

Some things, like a cask of wine, can be exploited immediately. The archers know Sir Geoffrey will permit this—it is only a fair reward, after all. But drunkenness is punishable, though Sir Geoffrey does not enforce that rule unless good supplies are ruined by a drunken lout or someone molests a person under Peel protection.

Once the tally is made, the soldiers may take their share, in whole or in part, from the captured goods if they fancy a particular item, or they may opt to take it in coin. Sir Geoffrey's purse may be strained to see that his soldiers' shares are paid out before the goods can be sold at market, but it is a strain he is willing to bear.

The day is theirs.

How Armor Changed:
Mail versus Plate

The harness of a man-at-arms changed notably during the course of the war, due in part to an arms race brought on by increasingly effective weapons and in part to improved metallurgy and consequently improved armoring skills. As the war progressed, better armor became more widely available.

In the early fourteenth century, English knights were armored much as their great-grandfathers had been. Their primary protection was mail ("chainmail" is a Victorian term, unknown to Sir Geoffrey), a fabric of interlocked rings. Each ring in the fabric connects to four others and is typically riveted closed. Sometimes a row of solid rings connects two rows of riveted rings.

Various garments can be made of mail, including shirts, hoods, mittens, and leg coverings. Such garments are tailored to achieve a snug fit; this both helps to reduce the considerable weight of mail armor and gives the wearer more freedom of movement. Tailoring can be achieved by inserting swatches of mail, often trapezoidal in shape, and by adding or dropping rings from the mesh, much as knitters expand or contract their work by adding or dropping stitches.

Mail is very resistant to sword cuts. However, its flexibility, while vital to the wearer's ability to move, is also its weakness. The impact of a blow is not spread efficiently, making mail somewhat vulnerable to a thrust or penetrating point. Also, a man's muscles can be bruised or his bones broken by a powerful blow, even one that fails to penetrate or break the mail armor.

Plate armor reacts quite differently to a blow. It spreads the force of a cutting edge or a striking point across its surface, making it less vulnerable to both crushing and penetrating forces.

Unlike mail, plate provides glancing surfaces, rounded shapes that can cause a blow to skitter across the plate rather than landing cleanly. The edges of a plate can be turned up to stop a point sliding across the surface from slipping past the edge and into the wearer.

The same rigidity that makes plate protective makes it far less flexible than mail. And since it is not a continuous fabric, each piece of a plate armor must be joined to the one next to it for full protection. Careful articulation between the plates is crucial if the wearer is to fight effectively. Armorers make this work by using various kinds of connection.

For the simple hinge joints of an armor (such as knees and elbows), one part is riveted directly to the parts above and below it. When rotational movement is needed (such as at the shoulders), parts are riveted to leather straps. The leather can flex, permitting the plates to ride over each other as the wearer moves.

The flexible leather strips connecting the parts of a shoulder defense are about to disappear as the piece is laced tight to the shoulder.

Just as mail's strength (flexibility) hides a weakness, plate's weakness (lack of flexibility) has a hidden value. Each harness comprises a number of separate elements. Each of these elements can have its own attachment point, allowing the weight of the harness to be borne by several points on the wearer's body. As a result, a given weight of plate armor is less burdensome to wear than the same weight of mail, most of which is carried on the shoulders.

Plate itself changed during the war, in more than styles and shaping. Toward the end of the fourteenth century, different types of steel were becoming more commonly available. In addition, armorers began to develop techniques for hardening armor plates. This allowed them to provide the same protection in a plate that was thinner and lighter than its predecessors.

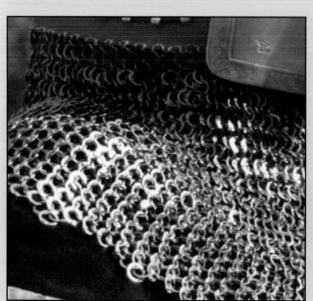

The lames (small plates) of an articulated elbow slide almost out of sight when the arm is straight, but close the gaps when the arm is bent.

The fabric of the mail aventail flows around Sir Geoffrey's neck and over his shoulder.

English knights were wearing old-fashioned armor at the start of the war. Many relied primarily on mail for protection. This knight, who could have accompanied Edward III on the first campaign of the war, is better equipped than some.

He wears a padded garment beneath his long-sleeved hauberk of mail. Over that, he has something that not all of his fellows wear: a poncho-like garment made of numerous small plates riveted to a foundation of cloth or, in his case, leather. He probably calls this garment a coat of plates, or simply "plates." Most of his torso protection is hidden under his old-fashioned cloth surcoat.

Poleyns cover his knees, and narrow strips of metal are hidden in the gamboised (quilted) cuisses on his thighs. His lower legs are protected by mail chausses, which cover his shoes as well.

A disk of plate called a besegew is laced to the sleeve of his hauberk. It is a small addition to the protection of the elbow. He wears a tight-fitting sleeve of mail on his lower arm, making for a double layer over most of his forearm. Many men are still wearing mittens of mail for hand protection. These might be separate items or they might be woven into the sleeves. Before battle, this knight will don a pair of gauntlets that consist of leather gloves to which many small, overlapping plates are riveted.

His helm is a style known as a heaume or great helm. The complex shape of the helm is achieved by riveting together plates of simple shape. The heaume has holes for breathing and a narrow slit for vision. It sits upon a smaller, close-fitting helmet to which is attached the aventail (a curtain of mail to protect the neck). It is a strong but, like his layered body armor, quite heavy.

He carries a shield (currently hung on his back using a strap called a guige) for additional protection, especially from arrows and lances. On horseback he will carry a lance. If he loses or breaks the lance, he will switch to a single-handed sword, which is also the weapon he uses when fighting on foot. It has a long, slightly tapered blade and is better for cutting or chopping blows than for thrusts.

The knight has removed his heaume, revealing the close-fitting helmet beneath. The heaume has a liner that rests on the helmet, but no fastenings. It relies on the close fit and its own weight to keep it in place.

The knight's lower arm is protected by a double layer of mail. A besegew, laced to the mail, adds protection for the outside of his elbow.

An English Knight circa 1346

This knight might have fought with the Prince of Wales at the battle of Crécy. He has more plate pieces than his predecessor, but he stills relies heavily on mail for protection.

The poleyns on his knees have been joined by shinbalds on his lower legs and the linked plates of solerets on the tops of his feet. All supplement his mail hosen.

His arm harness is also more developed. The vambrace, a pair of hinged plates, fully encloses his forearm and provides much improved protection for his vulnerable forearm. Leather gloves with small, overlapping plates riveted to them protect his hands. Fingers, hand, and wrist remain vulnerable to a crushing blow.

His helmet is a more elaborate version of the small helmet worn under a great helm. Some men are still wearing heaumes into battle, but this knight is not one of them. He prefers to fight with his face exposed, allowing him better vision and easier breathing.

His outer cloth garment is a cyclas. It is similar to the earlier surcoat, but more closely fitted, and the front of the skirt has been shortened. The change may make it easier to fight on foot—or it may simply be a change of fashion.

The cut of the cyclas reveals the layers of armor protecting his torso. Like his predecessor, he wears a padded garment and over that a full mail shirt, and a coat of plates. Unlike his predecessor, his coat of plates includes lappets, strips of leather reinforced with plates of metal that extend down from his waist to protect his lower torso.

In battle, he still carries a shield, whether on horseback or afoot. His weapons are are the same as his predecessor's, but his sword is of a type just coming into vogue. The tapered blade makes it notably better for thrusting while still retaining a dangerous cutting capacity.

After the great victory at Crécy, English men-at-arms will want improved armor, with the technical advances they have seen in French armor. And with the influx of wealth from French spoils and ransoms, most English knights will be able to afford modern armor.

The many plates of the gauntlet offer flexibility but make for a heavy piece of armor. Later gauntlets evolve the coverage of the wrist and back of the hand to a single, cunningly curved plate.

A variety of points and straps hold the elements of the arm armor in place. A leather tab riveted beneath the shoulder cap allows it to be laced to the mail shirt. The upper armor plate has lacing holes at its top and is secured to the arm by a pair of straps. The elbow disk is laced to the couter, using the point that spans the inside of the elbow and holds both pieces in place. The vambrace is pointed near the elbow to the sleeve of the padded garment below. A single strap keeps it closed.

By the middle of the century, fashions have changed and armor has changed as well. A more tightly fitting garment underlies the armor. It may be called a doublet, aketon, gambeson, jupon, or pourpoint—terminology is neither systematic nor consistent. Whatever its name, it is stoutly constructed. Multiple layers of cloth absorb impacts, soak up sweat, protect the wearer from chafing, and offer some protection from blows that penetrate the metal armor. The gambeson is typically laced tightly at the waist to distribute the weight of the leg harness tied to it. The upper portions are looser, and cunningly tailored to allow free movement of the knight's arms.

The skirt and sleeves of his mail shirt have been shortened to make it a haubergeon (little hauberk). Over that he might wear a more sophisticated version of the coat of plates, with fewer and larger plates protecting the body. He might wear a breastplate. Whatever additional chest protection he chooses, it will be shaped to give him a fashionable silhouette.

Over his torso protection, he wears a cloth garment of the style sometimes called a jupon. This may be simply a layer or two of colorful cloth or it may be padded for additional protection.

His helmet is a visored bascinet, a style that will be the most common form for the rest of the century and well into the next. A visor offers full face protection, but also allows the knight a chance to grab a quick breath of fresh air or a fast, unimpeded look around.

His legs and arms are completely encased in metal. The armor for each limb makes a single, jointed assembly of armor. His hands and feet have their own plate armor. Sabatons cover his shoes on top, leaving the shoe sole unprotected so that his feet get a good grip upon the ground. Gauntlets, which have taken on the hour-glass design that will be standard for over fifty years, protect his hands. The part covering the back of the hand and the wrist is a single plate. The fingers remain overlapped plates riveted to leather strips.

He no longer carries a shield, except in mounted combat where the extra protection still makes a difference against a lance. On foot, he will be fighting with a weapon that uses two hands, either a spear (sometimes quickly fashioned from a lance cut down to a length more handy for fighting on foot) or the long-hilted sword of war that can be gripped with one or both hands.

This knight (above) has reversed the usual arrangement and wears his breastplate beneath his mail shirt.

This knight's arm harness is a single, jointed assembly. The shoulder cap and its lames are attached to each other and the upper arm by leather strips on the inside. This allows rotational movement. The upper and lower arm pieces are riveted to the lames that connect them to the elbow protection. This is a stronger join, but one which limits movement to a simple hinging action.

An English Knight circa 1415

About the end of the fourteenth century, men-at-arms discard the cloth covering for their armor, beginning what armor historians call the white harness period, named for the bright "white" metal of the armor. With no cloth covering it, the full plate protection for the torso is now entirely visible.

Occasionally after this point, new forms of cloth covering will come into use, but not for very long, nor will they be adopted by most fighting men.

The upper torso is protected by a cuirass, a close fitting protection made of two large pieces of curved metal. The breastplate covers the front and the backplate the rear.

Also now visible is the protection for the lower torso: a hooped skirt. The fauld (front section) is attached to the breastplate and the cullet (back section) is attached to the backplate. Each lame of the fauld and cullet is attached to leather straps, a system that gives the necessary flexibility to bend and sit.

A knight still needs protection on the inside of his joints and under the armpits, as well as coverage for the gap between the torso and leg armor. Some knights still wear a complete mail shirt beneath the plate armor. Others wear a long-sleeved, vest-like shirt that comes just below the arm openings of the plate. They then tie on a short, separate skirt of mail at the waist. A few may even be using an arming coat, as is common by the end of the war.

Notable changes in protection come from the modified helm and from the besegews, now positioned to provide extra protection for the vulnerable armpit area.

This knight wears a great bascinet, a helmet derived from the visored bascinet so common earlier. The shape of the skull and the visor remain similar, but the aventail of mail has been replaced by pieces of plate. It is much more protective of the neck, but it restricts neck motion notably more than mail does. Beneath it, he wears a mail standard, a tight-fitting collar with a short cape. The edges of the cape can sometimes be seen peeking out from beneath the plate neckguard.

A great bascinet's close fit and rigid neck protection make it tricky to slip in and out of.

The alternative helmet shown here features movable plates to protect the chin. This allows the helmet to fit tightly, yet still permits the wearer to get it on and off easily. It is a system that will develop more fully in the armet.

By the end of the war, plate armor defenses are essentially complete. Refinements will continue to be made and styles change, but by this time armorers have achieved near complete and successful coverage.

One of the biggest changes is the adoption of an arming coat, the latest version of the padded garment worn beneath armor. Selected pieces of mail are sewn or laced to it, to cover the gaps in the plate. Using mail only where absolutely necessary is much lighter and less cumbersome than wearing a full shirt of mail.

Over his arming doublet, this knight wears a cuirass of plate. It has curved, cleverly-shaped large plates to armor the upper torso. The breastplate has a fixture for an arrêt, a device to help steady a lance. His hips are covered by a fauld and cullet. Additional plates called tassets are strapped to the fauld to help cover the gap between it and the leg armor.

His limbs are covered in plate. Wide, flaring plates help protect the inside of the elbow, and the close-fitting shoulder armor of Sir Geoffrey's day has been replaced with pauldrons that enfold the shoulder region and offer much better coverage for the vulnerable armpits.

Another notable change has occurred in the gauntlets. The plates covering the fingers have merged together, almost like mittens. While this affords less flexibility, it provides far more protection, especially from heavy, crushing blows.

The helmet he wears is an armet. It is an advance on the bascinet and aventail worn by Sir Geoffrey. Hinged plates allow it to be both close-fitting and easy to put on and off. Even with the visor raised, the lower face remains protected. This one is fitted with a bevor which reinforces the lower face and covers the neck opening. Other styles of helmet have come into use as well, but the armet is popular with the English.

Shields have long since fallen out of favor for all but mounted combat. Armor is very protective and a shield gets in the way when using two-handed weapons, needed for fighting a well armored man. This knight is using a poll ax. It is essentially the same weapon preferred by Sir Geoffrey, but this one is even more specialized for dealing with plate armor. He also carries a longsword and a dagger.

Even with the armet's visor raised, little of the face is exposed.

A detail of the knight's gauntlets. The round metal disk near the shaft of the poll-ax is actually part of the weapon and not the right-hand gauntlet.

APPENDIX

Glossary

abbey: a self-governing monastery

abbot: superior of an abbey

abstinence: religious discipline: avoiding prohibited foods (meat, poultry, eggs, dairy products), especially on designated days

Advent: season of preparation for Christmas

affinity: men and women within a lord's patronage

aketon: body armor of padded cloth

almshouse: charitable home for the poor

alum: common mordant

arable: suitable for farming

arming sword: sword carried by a man in armor

aumbry: cupboard

Ave Maria: "Hail Mary" prayer; in the fourteenth century, only the Biblical portion

aventail: curtain of mail suspended from the helm to protect the neck

bascinet: close-fitting helmet, possibly with a visor

battle (*bataille*): main division of a medieval army

beadle: minor law enforcment officer

bevor: lower-face armor

benefice: salaried church office

bishop: senior official of the Church, head of a diocese

Blessed Virgin: Mary, the mother of Jesus

bodger: itinerant wood-turner

braes: man's drawers

braegirdle: belt over the braes, to keep them up and/ or provide attachment places for hosen

brigandine: body armor of small plates riveted into a cloth garment

budge: lambskin used as a fur

canon: (1) the rules of a religious order; (2) priest living communally under such a rule

cautery: burning the flesh, for example with a hot iron

chantry: privately funded liturgy, usually a series of Masses for the dead

chapelle de fer: helmet with a brim and open face (from the French, "iron hat")

chevage: fee for permission to live away from the manor

chevauchée: destructive cavalry raid

chivalry: (1) the knightly class; (2) the institution of knighthood; (3) the virtues and traits associated with knights

cobbler: shoe repairer

cog: cargo ship with sails but no oars

coif: man's head covering, old-fashioned by 1381

collation: snack or light meal, particularly on fast days

common, commoner: one without rank or status; the vast majority of Englishmen

coney: rabbit

coppice: (1) cut down a tree to permit shoots to grow from the stump; see pollard; (2) the shoots of a coppiced tree

cordwainer: shoemaker

corn: leading crop of an area

Corpus Christi: (1) Body of Christ; (2) the holy day dedicated to honoring it

costrel: flask, usually of pottery or leather, with loops to attach carrying cords

cotton wool: unspun cotton, used for padding in men's doublets and armoring clothes

coulter: blade at the front of a plow that slices the soil vertically (see plowshare)

courser: war horse, lighter and nimbler than a destrier, popular later in the century

couter: elbow armor

cuirass: body armor comprising breastplate and backplate

cuisse: thigh armor

cullet: armor for the back of the hips, of lames riveted to leather straps

cupping: drawing blood by placing heated cups over small cuts in the patient's skin; they create a slight vacuum as they cool, which sucks out small amounts of blood

curfew: pottery cover for a fire, to keep the embers smoldering overnight

dagged: scalloped

deed of arms: armed encounter

destrier: heavy war horse, popular early in the century

diocese: bishop's jurisdiction, a territory and its churches

divine office: daily prayers and readings performed by religious communities

downs: hills or uplands; in Hampshire, consisting primarily of chalk soil

egredouce: sweet and sour sauce

estate: station in life; see three estates

fairing: souvenir or gift from a fair

fasting: religious discipline: restricting the number and size of meals, especially on designated days

fauld: armor for the front of the hips, of lames riveted to leather straps

fell: skin, specifically of a sheep

feudal levy: royal summons to vassals owing military service

fewmets: deer droppings

fish day: day of abstinence

fosterling: child of gentle birth being raised in the household someone other than its parents

fraternity: organization of laypeople for social service and mutual support

frieze: coarse wool cloth

friar: itinerant preacher who lives by begging

free company: organized band of *routiers*

frontlet: decorative band worn across the forehead

frieze: heavy, coarse wool

full: beat or tread cloth to clean or thicken it

gambeson: padded under-armor garment

gauntlet: metal glove

gazehound: dog that hunts by sight rather than by scent

gentle, gentry: somewhat vague and mutable class between the commons and the nobility

girdle: belt

gown: top garment for both men and women; often more formal or rich than the garment beneath

grande assiette: "big armhole," a sleeve style permitting a wide range of arm movement

great helm: enclosed helm that covers the head and neck

greave: lower-leg armor

groom: lower-level man-servant

guild: see fraternity; also an organization of practitioners of a craft

harness: collective term for a man-at-arms's armor

haubergeon: short mail shirt

hauberk: long mail shirt

havoc: signal for pillage to begin

haws: fruits of hawthorns

hearth tax: "per-household" tax, as opposed to taxes on individuals or properties (see poll tax)

heaume: great helm

heriot: fine due to the lord on the death of a tenant

hips: fruits of roses

hobby: small horse

hoggaster: young sheep

Holy Week: week before Easter

huckster: small retailer, especially of produce or prepared food

humors: four essential body fluids (blood, phlegm, yellow bile, and black bile) which must be kept in balance for good health

hurdle: portable fence of woven sticks

indenture: contract

journeyman: craftsman who is paid a daily wage

jupon: sleeveless, fitted over-armor garment

juste à pie: joust on foot

kebb: weak or sickly sheep

kermes: Mediterranean insects which yield a rich red dye

kirtle: woman's underdress, the layer between smock and gown; may be worn without the gown informally or in warm weather

lactage: fee for the rental of a milking ewe

lame: small plate or strip of metal, usually assembled in groups as part of a harness

latten: alloy of copper

lay brother/sister: member of a religous community who was responsible for manual or administrative rather than spiritual labor

Lent: forty days before Easter, a season of repentance and self-denial

liripipe: long tail of a hood

longsword: sword with relatively long blade and grip, generally for two-handed use

mainward: center battle of an army

man-at-arms: fully-armored soldier capable of fighting either from horse or on foot

Mass: primary liturgy of the Roman Church

mead: fermented honey beverage

merchet: fee for a child's marriage, paid by a tenant to the lord

merels (nine-men's morris): board game for two players, see page 170

messuage: house with its associated land

Michaelmas: September 29, the Feast of St. Michael the Archangel; the official end of harvest and the fiscal year

miniver: fur of Russian squirrels; "pured" miniver is the white belly fur, with all gray body fur trimmed away

monastery: house of monks

monk: member of a cloistered community or an order of hermits

mordant: dye fixative

multure: share of milled grain paid to the miller as his fee

mutton: meat of mature sheep (as opposed to lamb)

nun: member of a religious order of women

opus anglicanum: "English work," embroidery, using primarily split stitch and couching

orle: thick ring of cloth serving as the base for a heraldic crest

pair: set (possibly more than two)

pair of plates: upper-body armor including both breast and back protection

palfrey: riding horse

Pater Noster: Our Father (The Lord's Prayer)

patis: permission to use the income of the region to pay expenses)

pell: man-sized target for combat practice

plowshare: larger blade of a plow that cuts the furrow (see coulter)

points: laces for attaching pieces of clothing or armor

poleyn: knee armor

poll tax: "per-head" tax, as opposed to taxes on households or properties (see hearth tax)

pollard: cut off the upper part of a tree to permit shoots to grow from the trunk; see coppice

popinjay: bird-shaped target for archery competitions

powder douce: mild or sweet spice mixture

powder forte: sharp spice mixture

quadrivium: arithmetic, geometry, music, and astronomy (see trivium)

quarrel: crossbow bolt or arrow

rearward: hindmost battle of an army

reeve: manorial officer, selected from among the villeins

regrator: retailer, specifically one who buys up goods before they come to market

routier, rutter: member of a band of discharged soldiers

rubrication: red lettering in a book or other manuscript

sabaton: flexible foot armor of multiple plates

samite: heavy silk twill fabric

scrip: satchel

shaw: strip of woodland between fields

shearer: cloth finisher

shed: in weaving, an open space between groups of warp threads

shive: pierced bung for a cask, plugged with a spile

shrive: absolve of sin, specifically through the sacrament of confession

side sword: sword that could be worn by one's side

smock: woman's inner garment, equivalent to a man's shirt

solar: private upstairs room

spile: wooden peg used to plug a shive

standard: (1) large tree that will be turned into timber; (2) standing collar of mail

sword of war: see longsword

tables: backgammon-like board game

tanner: craftsman who makes hide into leather

teasel: variety of thistle with hooked prickles, used to comb fiber or raise the nap on cloth

thatcher: itinerant roofer, working in reeds or straw

three estates: those who fight (knights and nobility), those who pray (clergy and religious), and those who work (everyone else)

toft: house's yard, garden, and outbuildings

tonsure: partly shaven head that designated professed clergy

trivium: Latin grammar, rhetoric, and logic; the foundation of all education (see quadrivium)

unshriven: not absolved of sin, particularly at the point of death

vambrace: lower-arm armor of plate

vanward: leading battle of an army

varlet: mid-level manservant

villein: man or woman bound to the land; serf

vintaine: military unit of twenty men

vintenar: captain of a vintaine

visor: hinged face protection for a helmet

vouge: polearm with a pronounced point at the blade's tip

warp: lengthwise threads in a piece of fabric

wayte: member of the municipal watch, who were secondarily musicians

weft: crosswise threads in a piece of fabric

wether: castrated sheep

white grease: lard

Gazetteer of Places Related to the Peel Household

THE MANOR AT DUNBURY is a construct based on facilities, events, and activities drawn from accounts of actual manors and is portrayed in this book by a number of sites. The manor house exterior and some of its interiors are Barley Hall, a York Archaeological Trust property in York, England. The Manor kitchen is in the Wine Merchant's House, an English Heritage property in Southampton, England. Various exterior locations, including the village well and parish churchyard, were shot at Prebendal Manor in Northamptonshire, England. Many other exteriors, including the Arundel homestead and the manor farmyards and pastures, were shot at the Weald and Downland Open Air Museum in Sussex, England. Some additional exteriors were shot at the Middelaldercentret in Nykøbing Falster, Denmark.

Middelaldercentret

Barley Hall

Prebendal Manor

Weald and Downland Open Air Museum

Wine Merchant's House

The RIVER TEST and HAMPSHIRE COUNTRYSIDE were primarily played by themselves, especially the river and the view from Danebury hill. Though it has changed from its medieval aspect, the verdant countryside can still evoke an earlier time.

The DUNBURY GREAT HALL, MARKET FAIR, and many exterior locations were staged within and on the grounds of "Nolan-Stern-Nolan Studios" in Virginia, USA thanks to the generosity and forbearance of two of La Belle Compagnie's long-standing members.

SOUTHAMPTON was played by itself in the case of the main city gate, Gerrit le Flemyng's town house, and one of the street scenes. The wider street shots come from The Weald and Downland Open Air Museum in Sussex, England, with additional backgrounds from the Middelaldercentret in Nykøbing Falster, Denmark.

Weald and Downland Open Air Museum

Middelaldercentret

Southampton

Historical People "Related" to the Peel Household

ANNE OF BOHEMIA (1366-94) The daughter of the Holy Roman Emperor Charles IV. She wed Richard II in 1382. When she died, a distraught Richard had the palace where she had died burned to the ground.

BERTRAND DU GUESCELIN (c.1320-1380) A rough-hewn Breton soldier who rose to become constable of France and Charles V's greatest general.

EDWARD III (1312-1377) King of England 1327-77. He instigated the Hundred Years War and led the English army to many of its early successes. By the time of his death, the French were retaking lost territory, and the English parliament was unwilling to continue funding an enterprise that had become unprofitable.

EDWARD OF WOODSTOCK (1330-1376) Prince of Wales and first son of Edward III. He won his spurs at 16 in the battle of Crécy and had a distinguished career as a warrior and general. He was renowned in his time as a paragon of chivalry and is known to history as the Black Prince.

FIORE DEI LIBERI (active c. 1380-1410) A fencing master and the author of the earliest surviving Italian manual of fence. His *Flos Duellatorum*, written in his old age at the start of the fifteenth century, is a comprehensive treatment of armed and unarmed combat.

GEOFFREY CHAUCER (c. 1340-1400) The son of a wine merchant, he served in France under Edward III and John of Lancaster, in Parliament, and as an esquire of the king's household. He held numerous positions in the royal administration, including as Controller of the Customs, diplomat, and Clerk of the Works; but his lasting renown is for poetry such as *Troilus and Criseyde* and the *Canterbury Tales*.

JOHN BALL (d. 1381) A priest with a long history of radical preaching, such as professing that all men were equal. He was an incendiary inspiration to the Revolt of 1381 and was hanged, drawn, and quartered for his part in it.

SIR JOHN HAWKWOOD (1320-1394) Professional soldier, son of an English tanner. He was knighted in France before joining the White Company, a band of *routiers* that fought profitably in the Italian wars. He became a famous captain, serving Florence from 1380, and retired honored and rich.

JOHN OF LANCASTER (JOHN OF GAUNT) (1340-1399) Second son of Edward III. He became duke of Lancaster through marriage to his first wife and gained a claim to the crown of Castile through his second. He spent much time and treasure trying to attain the Castilian throne. In 1381, he was probably the most powerful individual in England – and very unpopular.

SIR JOHN STRATTON (active 1350-1390) Constable of Bordeaux 1381-87, seneschal of Gascony 1382-83. Arrived in Gascony with the Black Prince in 1355 and settled there.

RICHARD II (1367-1399) Son of Edward of Woodstock, King of England 1377-99. The early promise of his reign was already eroded when he assumed full power in 1389; he was deposed in 1399 by Henry Bolingbroke, son of John of Lancaster. He died (or was murdered) that year in imprisonment.

SIR ROBERT KNOLLYS (KNOLLES) (d. 1407) Born a commoner, he probably began his military career as an archer. He ended it as one of the most feared English captains of his time.

SIR ROBERT PASSELEWE and SIR PETER LE VEEL The two knights who were charged by Richard II with suppressing all signs of revolt in Hampshire and Wiltshire following the Revolt of 1381.

SIMON OF SUDBURY (d. 1381) Archbishop of Canterbury 1375-81, chancellor of England 1380-81. During the Revolt of 1381 the mob dragged him and ROBERT HALES (prior of St. Johns, newly appointed Treasurer) from the Tower of London and beheaded them.

WAT TYLER (d. 1381) A man of uncertain origins, one of the leaders of the Revolt of 1381. He was killed under questionable circumstances, during or after a parley with the king.

Prayers in Latin and Englysh

Pater Noster

Pater noster, qui es in caelis, sanctificetur nomen tuum.	Oure fadir that art in heuenes, halewid be thi name.
Adveniat regnum tuum.	Come to thi kingdom.
Fiat voluntas tua, sicut in caelo et in terra.	Thi wille be don in erthe, and as it is in heuene.
Panem nostrum quotidianum da nobis hodie,	Oure ech daies breed gyue us to-dai,
et dimitte nobis debita nostra,	and forgyue us oure dettis,
sicut et nos dimittimus debitoribus nostris.	as and we forgyuen to our dettouris
Et ne nos inducas in tentationem:	and lede us not in-to temptacioun;
sed libera nos a malo.	but delyuere us from yuel.
Amen.	Amen.

Ave Maria

Ave Maria, gratia plena, Dominus tecum.	Heil, marie, ful of grace, the lord is with thee.
Benedicta tu in mulieribus,	blessid be thou among wymmen,
et benedictus fructus ventris tui, Jesus.	and blessid be the fruyt of thi wombe, Ihesus.

Bibliography –
An Introduction to the Period

Agriculture

Hartley, Dorothy. *Lost Country Life*. New York: Pantheon Books 1979

Arms, Armor, and Military Matters

Barber, Richard. *The Reign of Chivalry*. New York: St. Martin's Press 1980

Barber, Richard. *The Knight and Chivalry*, revised edition. Woodbridge: The Boydell Press 1995

Bartlett, Clive & Gerry Embleton. *English Longbowman 1330-1515*, 2nd edition. London: Osprey 1997

Bradbury, Jim. *The Medieval Siege*. Woodbridge: The Boydell Press 1992

Edge, David & John Miles Paddock. *Arms & Armor of the Medieval Knight*. New York: Crescent 1988

Gravett, Christopher. *English Medieval Knight 1300-1400*. London: Osprey 2002

Hardy, Robert. *Longbow: A social and military history*, 3rd edition. Yeovil: Haynes 2006

Art and Illumination

"*In Medieval Manuscripts*" series. Toronto: University of Toronto Press

Biography

Hicks, Michael. *Who's Who in Late Medieval England*. London: Shepheard-Walwyn 1991

Daily Life

Gies, Frances & Joseph. *Marriage and the Family in the Middle Ages*. New York: Harper & Row 1987

Gies, Joseph & Frances. *Life in a Medieval Castle*. New York: Harper & Row 1979

Gies, Joseph & Frances. *Life in a Medieval City*. New York: Harper & Row 1981

Singman, Jeffrey L., & Will McLean. *Daily Life in Chaucer's England*. Westport: Greenwood 1995

Keen, Maurice. *English Society in the Later Middle Ages 1348-1500*. New York: Penguin 1990

Food

Butler, Sharon & Constance B. Hieatt. *Pleyn Delit*. Toronto: University of Toronto Press 1987

Heraldry

Neubecker, Ottfried. *Heraldry: Sources, Symbols, and Meaning*. Maidenhead: McGraw-Hill 1976

Reeves, Compton. *Pleasure and Pastimes in Medieval England*. Oxford: Oxford University Press 1998

Rowling, Marjorie. *Everyday Life in Medieval Times*. London: Batsford 1968

Rowling, Marjorie. *Everyday Life of Medieval Travellers*. New York: Dorset Press 1989

What Life Was Like in the Age of Chivalry. Alexandria: Time-Life Books 1997

History

Collins, Marie & Virginia Davis. *A Medieval Book of Seasons*. New York: HarperCollins 1992

Cowie, Richard. *The Black Death and Peasants' Revolt*. New York: Putnam 1972

Fowler, Kenneth. *The Age of Plantagenet and Valois: The Struggle for Supremacy 1328-1498*. London: Elek 1967

Tuchman, Barbara W. *A Distant Mirror: The Calamitous Fourteenth Century*. New York: Knopf 1978

Religion

Hamilton, Bernard. *Religion in the Medieval West*, 2nd edition. London: Edward Arnold 2003

Trades and Crafts

Medieval Craftsmen series. London: British Museum Press

Women

Coss, Peter. *The Lady in Medieval England 1000-1500*. Mechanicsburg: Stackpole Books 1998

Uitz, Erika, trans. Sheila Marnie. *The Legend of Good Women: Medieval Women in Towns & Cities*. Mount Kisco: Moyer Bell Limited 1990

Bibliography - For Further Reading

Agriculture

Crane, Eva. *The Archaeology of Beekeeping.* London: Duckworth 1983

Crowther, R. E. & J. Evans. *Coppice*, 2nd edition. London: Her Majesty's Stationery Office 1986

Henisch, Bridget Ann. *The Medieval Calendar Year.* University Park: Pennsylvania State University Press 1999

Landsberg, Sylvia. *The Medieval Garden.* New York: Thames and Hudson 1995

Miller, Edward, ed. *The Agrarian History of England and Wales, vol. 3 1348-1500.* Cambridge: Cambridge University Press 1991

Sweeney, Del. *Agriculture in the Middle Ages.* Philadelphia: University of Pennsylvania Press 1995

Arms, Armor, and Military Matters

Anglo, Sydney. *The Martial Arts of Renaissance Europe.* New Haven: Yale University Press 2000

Ascham, Roger, ed. Peter E. Medine. *Toxophilus.* Tempe: Arizona Center for Medieval and Renaissance Studies 2002

Ayton, Andrew. *Knights and Warhorses: Military Service and the English Aristocracy Under Edward III.* Woodbridge: The Boydell Press 1994

Barber, Richard. *The Life and Campaigns of the Black Prince from Contemporary Letters, Diaries, and Chronicles.* London: Folio Society 1979

Barber, Richard & Juliet Barker. *Tournaments: Jousts, Chivalry and Pageants in the Middle Ages.* New York: Weidenfeld & Nicolson 1898

Barker, Juliet R. V. *The Tournament in England, 1100-1400.* Woodbridge: The Boydell Press 1986

Barnie, John. *War in Medieval English Society: Social Values and the Hundred Years War 1337-99.* Ithaca: Cornell University Press 1974

Blair, Claude. *European Armour.* London: Batsford 1958

Bradbury, Jim. *The Medieval Archer.* New York: St. Martin's Press 1985

Burne, Alfred H. *The Crécy War.* Ware: Wordsworth Editions 1999

Coopland, G. W. *The Tree of Battles of Honoré Bonet.* Liverpool: University Press of Liverpool 1949

Coss, Peter. *The Knight in Medieval England 1000-1400.* Stroud: Sutton 1993

Curry, Ann & Michael Hughes, ed. *Arms, Armies and Fortifications of the Hundred Years War.* Woodbridge: The Boydell Press 1994

Davis, R. H. C. *The Medieval Warhorse.* New York: Thames and Hudson 1989

de Charny, Geoffroi, trans. Richard W. Kaeuper & Elspeth Kennedy. *The Book of Chivalry.* University Park: Pennsylvania State University Press 1996

de Pizan, Christine, trans. Sumner Willard, ed. Charity Cannon Willard. *The Book of Deeds of Arms and of Chivalry.* University Park: Pennsylvania State University Press 1999

Delbrück, Hans, trans. Walter J. Renfroe, Jr. *Medieval Warfare.* Lincoln: University of Nebraska Press 1990

DeVries, Kelly. *Medieval Military Technology.* Orchard Park: Broadview Press 1992

DeVries, Kelly. *Infantry Warfare in the Early Fourteenth Century.* Woodbridge: The Boydell Press 1996

ffoulkes, Charles. *The Armourer and his Craft.* New York: Dover 1989

Gravett, Christopher. *The World of the Medieval Knight.* New York: Peter Bedrick 1996

Hardy, Robert. *The Great Warbow.* Stroud: Sutton 2005

Howard, Michael, George J. Andreopoulos, & Mark R. Shulman, ed. *The Laws of War.* New Haven: Yale University Press 1994

Hyland, Anne. *The Medieval Warhorse: From Byzantium to the Crusades.* Stroud: Sutton 1994

Hyland, Anne. *The Warhorse 1250-1600.* Stroud: Sutton 1998

Koch, H. W. *Medieval Warfare.* London: Prentice Hall 1978

Flavius Vegetius Renatus, trans. N. P. Milner. *Vegetius: Epitome of Military Science.* Liverpool: Liverpool University Press 1993

Muhlberger, Steven. *Jousts and Tournaments: Charny and the Rules for Chivalric Sport in Fourteenth Century France.* Union City: The Chivalry Bookshelf 2002

Nicolle, David. *Medieval Warfare Source Book.* London: Arms and Armour 1995

Norris, John. *Early Gunpowder Artillery c. 1300-1600.* Marlborough: The Crowood Press 2000

Oakeshott, R. Ewart. *Records of the Medieval Sword.* Woodbridge: The Boydell Press 1991

Oakeshott, R. Ewart. *The Sword in the Age of Chivalry.* Woodbridge: The Boydell Press 1991

Oakeshott, R. Ewart. *The Archaeology of Weapons.* London: Lutterworth Press 1960

Oman, C.W.C., ed. John H. Beeler *The Art of War in the Middle Ages*, revised edition. Ithaca: Cornell University Press 1953

Powicke, Michael. *Military Obligation in Medieval England.* Oxford: Clarendon 1996

Prestwich, Michael. *Armies and Warfare in the Middle Ages: The English Experience.* New Haven: Yale University Press 1996

Price, Brian R. *Techniques of Medieval Armour Reproduction: the 14th Century.* Boulder: Paladin Press 2000

Reid, William. *Arms Through the Ages.* New York: Harper & Row 1976

Robards, Brooks. *The Medieval Knight at War.* New York: Barnes & Noble 1997

Seward, Desmond. *The Hundred Years War: The English in France, 1337-1453.* New York: Atheneum 1978

Soar, Hugh D. H. *The Crooked Stick: A History of the Longbow.* Yardley: Westholme 2004

Sumption, Jonathan. *The Hundred Years War I: Trial by Battle.* Philadelphia: University of Pennsylvania Press 1990

Sumption, Jonathan. *The Hundred Years War II: Trial by Fire.* Philadelphia: University of Pennsylvania Press 1999

Trapp, Oswald Graf. *The Armoury of the Castle of Churburg.* London: Methuen 1929

Art and Illumination

Avril, Françoise. *Manuscript Painting at the Court of France: The Fourteenth Century.* New York: Braziller 1978

Backhouse, Janet. *The Luttrell Psalter.* London: The British Library 1969

Backhouse, Janet. *The Illuminated Page.* Toronto: University of Toronto Press 1997

Camille, Michael. *The Gothic Idol: Ideology and Image-making in Medieval Art.* Cambridge: Cambridge University Press 1991

Camille, Michael. *Image on the Edge: The Margins of Medieval Art.* Chicago: Reaktion 1992

Camille, Michael. *Master of Death.* New Haven: Yale University Press 1996

Camille, Michael. *Mirror in Parchment: The Luttrell Psalter and the making of Medieval England.* Chicago: University of Chicago Press 1998

Cutler, Charles D. *Northern Painting from Pucelle to Bruegel.* New York: Holt, Reinhart, and Wilson 1968

de Hamel, Christopher. *A History of Illuminated Manuscripts.* London: Phaidon 1994

Dunkerton, Jill, Susan Foister, Dillian Gordon, Nicholas Penny. *Giotto to Dürer: Early Renaissance Painting in the National Gallery.* New Haven: Yale University Press 1991

Hedeman, Anne D. *The Royal Image: Illustrations of the Grandes Chroniques de France 1274-1422.* Berkeley: University of California Press 1996

The Hours of Jeanne d'Evreux, Queen of France. New York: Metropolitan Museum of Art 1957

The Hunting Book of Gaston Phébus. London: Harvey Miller 1998

Longuon, Jean & Raymond Cazelles, ed. *The Tres Riches Heures of Jean, Duke of Berry.* New York: Braziller 1969

Marcel, Thomas. *The Golden Age: Manuscript Painting at the Time of Jean, Duke of Berry.* New York: Braziller 1979

Marcel, Thomas. *The Rohan Master: A Book of Hours.* New York: Braziller 1973

Marks, Richard & N. J. Morgan. *The Golden Age of English Manuscript Painting 1200-1500.* New York: Braziller 1981

Meiss, Millard. *French Painting in the Time of Jean de Berry: The Limbourgs and Their Contemporaries.* New York: Braziller 1974

Meiss, Millard & Elizabeth Beatson, ed. *The Belles Heures of Jean, Duke of Berry.* New York: Braziller 1974

Meiss, Millard. *French Painting in the Time of Jean de Berry: The Late XIV Century and the Patronage of the Duke.* London: Phaidon 1967

Pirani, Emma. *Gothic Illuminated Manuscripts.* London: Hamlyn 1966

Rouse, E. Clive. *Medieval Wall Paintings,* 4th edition. Princes Risborough: Shire 1991

Sherman, Claire Richter. *The Portraits of Charles V of France (1338-1380).* New York: New York University Press 1969

Snyder, James. *Medieval Art.* New York: Prentice Hall 1989

Stone, Lawrence. *Sculpture in Britain: The Middle Ages,* 2nd edition. Harmondsworth: Pelican History of Art series 1972

Suckale, Robert & Matthias Weniger, ed. Ingo R. Walther. *Painting of the Gothic Era.* Cologne: Taschen 1999

Walters Art Gallery. *The International Style: The Arts in Europe around 1400.* Baltimore: Walters Art Gallery 1962

Spenser, J., trans. *The Four Seasons of the House of Cerruti.* New York: Facts on File 1984

Biography

Barber, Richard. *Edward Prince of Wales and Aquitaine: A Biography of the Black Prince.* London: Allen Lane 1978

Bevan, Bryan. *Edward III.* London: Rubicon Press 1992

Bevan, Bryan. *King Richard II.* London: Rubicon 1990

de Silva-Vigier, Anil. *This Moste Highe Prince John of Gaunt.* Durham: Pentland Press 1992

Howard, Donald R. *Chaucer: His Life, His Works, His World.* New York: Fawcett 1987

Saul, Nigel. *Richard II.* New Haven: Yale University Press 1997

Buildings

Fossier, Jean Chapelot Robert, trans. Henry Cleere. *The Village & House in the Middle Ages.* Berkeley: University of California Press 1985

Grenville, Jane. *Medieval Housing.* London: Leicester University Press 1997

Wood, Margaret. *The English Mediaeval House.* London: Bracken Books 1990

Commerce

Bennet, Judith M. *Ale, Beer, and Brewsters in England.* Oxford: Oxford University Press 1996

Cameron, David Kerr. *The English Fair.* Stroud: Sutton 1998

Dyer, Christopher. *Making a Living in the Middle Ages.* New Haven: Yale University Press 2002

Gies, Frances & Joseph. *Cathedral, Forge, and Waterwheel.* New York: HarperCollins 1994

Hunt, Edwin S. & James M. Murray. *A History of Business in Medieval Europe, 1200-1500.* Cambridge: Cambridge University Press 1999

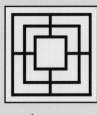

The Rules of Merels

Each player starts with nine pieces.

Players take turns laying pieces on intersections or corners.

Three pieces in a line is a "mill." Mills can be formed lengthwise or crosswise but not diagonally.

When a player makes a mill, she may take away one of the other player's pieces—but not from a mill.

When all the pieces are on the board, players take turns moving pieces. A move is sliding one piece along a line to the next empty corner or cross. Players may not skip a space or jump over a piece.

When one player has only two pieces left, or cannot move any pieces, the other player is the winner.

If both players can move but neither can make a mill, the player with the most pieces left is the winner.

Hutchinson, Gillian. *Medieval Ships and Shipping.* Rutherford: Fairleigh Dickinson University Press 1994

Power, Eileen. *The Wool Trade in English Medieval History.* London: Oxford University Press 1965

Spufford, Peter. *Money and Its Use in Medieval Europe.* Cambridge: The Stationery Office 1988

Costume and Adornment

Arnold, Janet. *The Jupon or Coat-Armour of the Black Prince in Canterbury Cathedral.* London: Journal of the Church Monuments Society Vol. VIII 1993

Beniss, Elijah. *The Dyer's Companion.* New York: Dover 1973

Bertram, Fr. Jerome, ed. *Monumental Brasses as Art and History.* Stroud: Sutton 1996

Bridbury, A. R. *Medieval English Clothmaking: An Economic Survey.* London: Heinemann Educational Books 1982

Burnham, Dorothy K. *Cut My Cote.* Toronto: Royal Ontario Museum 1973

Bury, Shirley. *An Introduction to Rings.* London: Stemmer House 1984

Clayton, Muriel. *Catalogue of Rubbings of Brasses and Incised Slabs.* London: Her Majesty's Stationery Office 1979

Davenport, Millia. *The Book of Costume.* New York: Crown 1984

Druitt, Herbert. *A Manual of Costume as Illustrated by Monumental Brasses.* Baltimore: Genealogical Publishing 1970

Evans, Joan. *Dress in Medieval France.* Oxford: Clarendon 1952

Fingerlin, Ilse. *Gürtel des hohen und späten Mittelalters.* Munich: Deutscher Kunstverlag 1971

Fischbach, Fredrick. *Historic Textile Patterns.* New York: Dover 1992

Geijer, A., A. N. Franzér, & M. Nockert. *Drottning Margarettas gullene kjortel (Queen Margaret's Golden Gown)* i Uppsala Domkyra. Stockholm: Kungl. Vitterhetsakademien 1985

Goubitz, Olaf, Carol van Driel-Murray, & Willy Groenman-van Waatering, trans. Olaf Goubitz & Xandra Barder. *Stepping Through Time.* Zwolle: Stichting Promotie Archeologie 2001

Harte, N.B., E. M. Carus-Wilson, & Kenneth G. Ponting, ed. *Cloth and Clothing in Medieval Europe.* London: Heinemann Educational Books 1983

Hodges, Laura F. *Chaucer and Costume: The Secular Pilgrims in the General Prologue.* Cambridge: Brewer 2000

Hurtig, Judith W. *The Armored Gisant Before 1400.* New York: Garland Publishing 1979

Lightbown, Ronald W. *Mediaeval European Jewelry.* London: Victoria & Albert Museum 1992

Liles, J. N. *The Art and Craft of Natural Dyeing.* Knoxville: University of Tennessee 1990

Martin, Rebecca. *Textiles in Daily Life in the Middle Ages.* Bloomington: Indiana University Press 1985

Mazzaoui, Maureen Fennell. *The Italian Cotton Industry in the Later Middle Ages 1100-1600.* Cambridge: Cambridge University Press 1981

Netherton, Robin & Gale R. Owen-Crocker, ed. *Medieval Clothing and Textiles, vols. 1, 2, 3* Woodbridge: The Boydell Press 2005-2007

Newton, Stella Mary. *Fashion in the Age of the Black Prince.* Woodbridge: The Boydell Press 1980

Nockert, Margareta. *Bockstensmannen.* Falkenberg: Foreningen Varsberg Museum 1985

Østergård, Else. *Woven into the Earth: Textiles from Norse Greenland.* Aarhus: Aarhus University Press 2004

Piponnier, Françoise & Perrine Mane, trans. Caroline Beamish. *Dress in the Middle Ages.* New Haven: Yale University Press 1997

Scott, Margaret. *A Visual History of Costume: The Fourteenth and Fifteenth Centuries.* London: Batsford 1986

Van Stralen, Trudy. *Indigo, Madder and Marigold.* Loveland: Interweave Press 1993

Veale, Elspeth M. *The English Fur Trade in the Later Middle Ages.* London: Oxford University Press 1966

Zijlstra-zweens, Henrika M. *Of His Array Telle I No Lenger Tale.* Amsterdam: Rodopi 1988

Daily Life

Arano, Luisa Cogliati. *The Medieval Health Handbook.* New York: Braziller 1976

Bisson, Lillian M. *Chaucer and the Late Medieval World.* New York: St. Martin's Press 1999

Blackley, P. D. & Gustav Hermansen. *The Household Book of Queen Isabella of England.* Edmonton: University of Alberta 1971

Blackmans, Wim, & Antheun Hanse, ed. *Showing Status: Representations of Social Positions in the Late Middle Ages.* Turnhout: Brepols 1999

Brewer, Derek. *Chaucer and His World.* New York: Dodd, Mead 1978

Brown, Michelle P. *A Guide to Western Historical Scripts from Antiquity to 1600.* Toronto: University of Toronto Press 1990

Chambers, R. W., & Walter W. Seton, ed. *A Fifteenth Century Courtesy Book.* London: Early English Text Society 1914

Clark, John, ed. *The Medieval Horse and Its Equipment.* London: Her Majesty's Stationery Office 1995

Collins, Marie & Virginia Davis. *A Medieval Home Companion.* New York: HarperCollins 1991

Cummins, John. *The Hound and the Hawk: The Art of Medieval Hunting.* New York: St. Martin's Press 1988

Songs About the Seasons

Sumer Is Icumen In

Sumer is icumen in,

lhude sing, cuccu.

Groweth sed and bloweth med

And springth the wude nu.

Sing, cuccu.

Awe bleteth after lomb,

Lhowth after calve cu.

Bulluc sterteth, bucke verteth,

Murye sing cuccu!

Cuccu, cuccu, wel singes thu cuccu,

Ne swik thu naver nu.

Summer is come in,

Loud sing cuckoo.

Seed grows and meadow blooms

And the wood sprouts anew.

Sing cuckoo!

The ewe bleats after the lamb,

The cow lows after the calf.

The bullock leaps, the buck farts,

Merry sing cuckoo!

Cuckoo, cuckoo, well you sing cuckoo,

Nor cease never now.

Miri It Is

Miri it is while sumer ilast

with fugheles song.

Oc nu necheth windes blast

And weder strong.

Ei, ei! What this nicht is long

And ich with wel michel wrong

Soregh and murne and fast.

Merry it is while summer lasts

with the birds' song.

But now come the wind's blasts

and storms are strong.

Oh, oh, this night is long

And I, enduring many a wrong,

Sorrow and mourn and fast.

de Worde, Wynkyn, ed. Anne Bagnall. *The Boke of Kervynge*. Lewes: Southover Press 2003

DeWindt, Edwin Brezette, ed. & trans. *A Slice of Life: Selected Documents of Medieval English Peasant Experience*. Kalamazoo: Medieval Institute Publications 1996

Duby, Georges, ed. *A History of Private Life, vol. 2: Revelations of the Medieval World*. Cambridge: Belknap 1988

Dyer, Christopher. *Standards of Living in the Later Middle Ages: Social Change in England c.1200-1520*. Cambridge: Cambridge University Press 1989

Dyer, Christopher. *Everyday Life in Medieval England*. London: Hambledon 1994

Dyer, Christopher. *An Age of Transition? Economy and Society in England in the Later Middle Ages*. Oxford: Clarendon 2005

Furnivall, F. J., ed. *The Babees Book*. London: Early English Text Society 1997

Goldberg, P.J.P. *Medieval England, A Social History 1250-1550*. London: Hodder Arnold 2004

Green, Monica H., ed. *The Trotula: A Medieval Compendium of Women's Medicine*. Philadelphia: University of Pennsylvania Press 2001

Hanawalt, Barbara A. *Growing up in Medieval London: The Experience of Childhood in History*. Oxford: Oxford University Press 1993

Herlihy, David. *Medieval Households*. Cambridge: Harvard University Press 1985

Hoffmann, Richard C. *Fisher's Craft & Lettered Art: Tracts on Fishing from the End of the Middle Ages*. Toronto: University of Toronto Press 1997

Hughes, Geoffrey. *Swearing: A Social History of Foul Language, Oaths and Profanity in English*. Oxford: Blackwell 1993

Hyland, Anne. *The Horse in the Middle Ages*. Stroud: Sutton 1999

Jusserand, Jean J., trans. Lucy Toulmin Smith. *English Wayfaring Life in the Middle Ages* (XIVth Century). London: Ernest Benn 1931

Le Goff, Jacques, trans. Arthur Goldhammer. *Time, Work, & Culture in the Middle Ages*. Chicago: University of Chicago Press 1982

Loomis, Roger Sherman. *A Mirror of Chaucer's World*. Princeton: Princeton University Press 1965

Milham, Mary Ella. *Platina: On Right Pleasure and Good Health*. Tempe: Medieval & Renaissance Texts & Studies 1998

Moriarty, Catherine. *The Voice of the Middle Ages in Personal Letters 1100-1500*. New York: Peter Bedrick 1989

Myers, A. R. *London in the Age of Chaucer*. Norman: University of Oklahoma 1972

Newman, Paul B. *Daily Life in the Middle Ages*. Jefferson: McFarland 2001

Ogden, Margaret Sinclair, ed. *The "Liber de Diversis Medicinis"*. London: Early English Text Society 1969

Ohler, Norbert, trans. Caroline Hillier. *The Medieval Traveller*. Woodbridge: The Boydell Press 1989

Origo, Iris. *The Merchant of Prato*. London: Folio Society 1984

Orme, Nicholas. *From Childhood to Chivalry: The Education of the English Kings and Aristocracy 1066-1530*. London: Methuen 1984

Orme, Nicholas. *Medieval Children*. New Haven: Yale University Press 2001

Orme, Nicholas. *Medieval Schools*. New Haven: Yale University Press 2006

Power, Eileen. *The Goodman of Paris*. Woodbridge: The Boydell Press 1928

Prescott, Andrew. *English Historical Documents*. London: The British Library 1988

Radulescu, Raluca & Alison Truelove, ed. *Gentry Culture in Late Medieval England*. Manchester: Manchester University Press 2005

Rawcliffe, Carole. *Medicine & Society in Later Medieval England*. Stroud: Sutton 1995

Rickert, Edith. *Chaucer's World*. New York: Oxford University Press 1948

Shahar, Shulamith. *Childhood in the Middle Ages*. London: Routledge 1992

Speed, Peter, ed. *Those who Fought*. New York: Italica 1996

Speed, Peter, ed. *Those who Prayed*. New York: Italica 1997

Speed, Peter, ed. *Those who Worked*. New York: Italica 1997

Thrupp, Sylvia L. *The Merchant Class of Medieval London*. Ann Arbor: University of Michigan Press 1989

Verdon, Jean, trans. George Holoch. *Travel in the Middle Ages*. Notre Dame: University of Notre Dame Press 2003

Webb, Diana. *Pilgrims and Pilgrimage in the Medieval West*. London: I. B. Tauris & Co Ltd 2001

Wilkins, Sally. *Sports and Games of Medieval Cultures*. Westport: Greenwood 2002

Woolgar, C. M., ed. *Household Accounts from Medieval England*. Oxford: Oxford University Press 1992

Food

Austin, Thomas, ed. *Two Fifteenth-Century Cookery-Books*. London: Early English Text Society 1996

Carlin, Martha & Joel T. Rosenthal, ed. *Foods and Eating in Medieval Europe*. London: Hambledon 1998

Hammond, P. W. *Food and Feast in Medieval England*. Stroud: Sutton 1993

Henisch, Bridget Ann. *Fast and Feast: Food in Medieval Society*. University Park: Pennsylvania State University 1996

Hieatt, Constance B. & Sharon Butler. *Curye on Inglysch*. London: Early English Text Society 1985

Hieatt, Constance B & Sharon Butler. *Pleyn Delit: Medieval Cookery for Modern Cooks*. Toronto: University of Toronto Press 1987

Hieatt, Constance B. *An Ordinance of Pottage*. London: Prospect Books 1988

Redon, Odile, Françoise Sabban, & Silvano Serventi. *The Medieval Kitchen*. Chicago: University of Chicago Press 1998

Sass, Lorna J. *To the King's Taste*. New York: The Metropolitan Museum of Art 1975

Scully, Terence. *The Art of Cookery in the Middle Ages*. Woodbridge: The Boydell Press 1977

Scully, Terence, ed. *The Vivendier: A Fifteenth Century French Cookery Manuscript*. London: Prospect Books 1997

Wilson, C. Anne. *Food and Drink in Britain*. Chicago: Academy Chicago 1991

Hampshire

Cantor, Leonard. *The English Medieval Landscape*. Philadelphia: University of Pennsylvania Press 1982

Cunliffe, Barry. *Dunbury*, revised edition. London: Batsford 1993

Hinton, David A. *Hampshire and the Isle of Wight*. London: George Philip & Son Ltd. 1988

Keene, Derek. *Survey of Medieval Winchester (Winchester Studies 2), vol. i and ii*. Oxford: Clarendon 1985

Platt, Colin. *Medieval Southampton: The Port and Trading Community AD 1000-1600*. London: Routledge & Kegan Paul 1973

Turner, Barbara Carpenter. *A History of Hampshire*. Stroud: Phillimore 1988

Heraldry

Foster, Joseph. *The Dictionary of Heraldry: Feudal Coats of Arms and Pedigrees.* London: Studio Editions 1996

Fox-Davies, Arthur. *The Art of Heraldry.* New York: Arno Press 1976

Pakula, Marvin H. *Heraldry and Armor of the Middle Ages.* Cranbury: A.S. Barnes 1972

History

Allmand, Christopher. *The Hundred Years War: England and France at War c. 1300-c. 1450.* Cambridge: Cambridge University Press 1988

Allmand, Christopher. *Society at War: The Experience of England and France during the Hundred Years War,* 2nd edition. Woodbridge: The Boydell Press 1998

Bean, J. M. W. *From Lord to Patron: Lordship in Late Medieval England.* Philadelphia: University of Pennsylvania Press 1989

Benedictow, Ole J. *The Black Death 1346-1353.* Woodbridge: The Boydell Press 2004

Britnell, Richard H. *The Commercialization of English Society 1000-1500,* 2nd edition. Manchester: Manchester University Press 1996

Cantor, Norman F *England c. 1200-1520.* Cambridge: Cambridge University Press 1989

Cantor, Norman F. *The Medieval Reader.* New York: HarperCollins 1994

Denholm-Young, N. *The Country Gentry in the Fourteenth Century.* Oxford: Clarendon 1969

Dobson, R. B., ed. *The Peasants' Revolt of 1381,* 2nd edition. Basingstoke: Macmillan 1983

Dunn, Alastair. *The Great Rising of 1381.* Charleston: Tempus 2002

Evans, Joan, ed. *The Flowering of the Middle Ages.* New York: Thames and Hudson 1998

Froissart, Jean, trans. Geoffrey Brereton. *Chronicles.* New York: Penguin 1978

Given-Wilson, Chris. *The Royal Household and the King's Affinity: Service, Politics and Finance in England 1360-1413.* New Haven: Yale University Press 1986

Given-Wilson, Chris. *The English Nobility in the Late Middle Ages.* London: Routledge & Kegan Paul 1987

Herlihy, David. *The Black Death and the Transformation of the West.* Cambridge: Harvard University Press 1997

Hicks, Michael. *Bastard Feudalism.* London: Longman 1995

Hilton, R. H. & T. H. Aston, ed. *The English Rising of 1381.* Cambridge: Cambridge University Press 1984

Hilton, Rodney. *Bond Men Made Free: Medieval Peasant Movements and the English Rising of 1381.* New York: Routledge 1986

Horrow, Rosemary, trans. & ed. *The Black Death.* Manchester: Manchester University Press 1994

Jones, Michael. *Ducal Brittany 1364-1399.* New York: Oxford University Press 1970

Labarge, Margaret Wade. *Gascony: England's First Colony 1204-1453.* London: Hamish Hamilton 1980

Le Goff, Jacques, ed., trans. Lydia G. Cochrane *The Medieval World.* London: Collins & Brown 1980

Matthew, Gervase. *The Court of Richard II.* London: John Murray 1968

McKisack, May. *The Fourteenth Century: 1307-1399.* Oxford: Oxford University Press 1991

Miller, Edward & John Hatcher. *Medieval England: Towns, Commerce and Crafts 1086-1348.* London: Longman 1995

Neilands, Robin. *The Hundred Years War.* London: Routledge 1991

Ormrod, W. M. *The Reign of Edward III: Crown & Political Society in England 1327-1377.* New Haven: Yale University Press 1990

Palmer, J. J. N. *England, France and Christendom, 1377-99.* Chapel Hill: University of North Carolina Press 1972

Platt, Colin. *Medieval England.* New York: Scribner 1978

Platt, Colin. *King Death.* Toronto: University of Toronto Press 1996

Siegler, Philip. *The Black Death.* New York: Harper & Row 1971

Tuck, Anthony. *Crown and Nobility 1272-1461: Political Conflict in Late Medieval England.* Totowa: Barnes & Noble 1986

Walker, Simon. *The Lancastrian Affinity 1361-1399.* Oxford: Oxford Historical Monographs 1990

Waugh, Scott L. *England in the Reign of Edward III.* Cambridge: Cambridge University Press 1991

Wright, Nicolas. *Knights and Peasants: The Hundred Years War in the French Countryside.* Woodbridge: The Boydell Press 1998

Wright, Silvia. *The Age of Chivalry: English Society 1200-1400.* New York: Warwick 1988

Literature

Anonymous, ed. J.R.R. Tolkien, E.V. Gordon, Norman Davis. *Sir Gawain and the Green Knight,* 2nd edition. Oxford: Oxford University Press 1987

Anonymous, ed. Derek Pearsall. *The Floure and the Leafe.* Kalamazoo: Medieval Institute Publications 1990

Chaucer, Geoffrey, ed. Walter W. Skeat. *The Legend of Good Women.* Oxford: Clarendon 1889

Chaucer, Geoffrey, ed. Donald R. Howard & James Dean. *Troilus and Criseyde and Selected Short Poems.* New York: Signet New American Library 1976

Chaucer, Geoffrey. *The Canterbury Tales.* New York: Avenel Books 1985

Kempe, Margery, trans. Barry Windeatt. *The Book of Margery Kempe.* New York: Penguin 1988

Krueger, Roberta L., ed. *The Cambridge Companion to Medieval Romance.* Cambridge: Cambridge University Press 2000

Langland, William, trans. J. F. Goodridge. *Piers the Plowman.* New York: Penguin 1987

Malory, Thomas. *Le Morte d'Arthur.* London: J. M. Dent & Sons 1967

Mandeville, John, trans. C. W. R. D. Moseley. *Travels.* New York: Penguin 1983

Manors and Tenants

Bailey, Mark, trans. *The English Manor c.1200-c.1500.* Manchester: Manchester University Press 2002

Bennett, H. S. *Life on the English Manor.* Cambridge: Cambridge University Press 1948

Britton, Edward. *The Community of the Vill: A Study of the History of the Family and Village Life in Fourteenth-Century England.* Toronto: Macmillan of Canada 1977

Fryde, E. B. *Peasants and Landlords in Later Medieval England.* Stroud: Sutton 1996

Hanawalt, Barbara A. *The Ties That Bound: Peasant Families in Medieval England.* New York: Oxford University Press 1986

Money

Farthing = 1/4 penny
Penny (plural = pence), written 1d
Groat = 4 pence

Shilling = 12 pence, written 1s
Mark = 2/3 pound (13 shillings, 4 pence)
Pound = 20 shillings = 240 pence, written £1

Hartley, Dorothy & Margaret M. Eliot. *Life and Work of the People of England: The Fourteenth Century*. New York: Putnam 1929

Hilton, R.H. *The English Peasantry in the Later Middle Ages*. Oxford: Clarendon 1979

Hooke, Della, ed. *Medieval Villages*. Oxford: Oxford University Press Committee for Archaeology 1985

Klingelhöfer, Eric. *Manor, Vill, and Hundred: The Development of Rural Institutions in Early Medieval Hampshire*. Toronto: Pontifical Institute of Medieval Studies 1992

Lock, Ray, ed. *The Court Rolls of Walsham le Willows 1351-99*. Woodbridge: The Boydell Press 2002

Raftis, J.A. *Peasant Economic Development Within the English Manorial System*. Stroud: Sutton 1996

Schofield, Phillipp R. *Peasant and Community in Medieval England 1200-1500*. New York: Palgrave Macmillan 2003

Woolgar, C. M. *The Great Household in Late Medieval England*. New Haven: Yale University Press 1999

Music

Cattin, Giulio, trans. Steven Botterill. *Music of the Middle Ages I*. Cambridge: Cambridge University Press 1984

Dobson, E.J. & F. L. Harrison *Medieval English Songs*. London: Faber & Faber 1979

Duffin, Ross W., Ed.. *A performer's Guide to Medieval Music*. Bloomongton: Indiana University Press 2002

Greenberg, Noah. *An English Song Book: part songs and sacred music of the Middle Ages and the Renaissance for one to six voices*. New York: Doubleday 1961

Hoppin, Richard H. *Medieval Music*. New York: Norton 1978

McGee, Timothy J. *Medieval Instrumental Dances*. Bloomington: Indiana University Press 1989

Munrow, David. *Instruments of the Middle Ages and Renaissance*. Oxford: Oxford UniversityPress 1976

Page, Christopher. *Voices and Instruments of the Middle Ages*. London: J. M. Dent & Sons 1987

Southworth, John. *The English Medieval Minstrel*. Woodbridge: The Boydell Press 1989

Wilkins, Nigel. *Music in the Age of Chaucer*. Cambridge: Brewer 1979

Objects and Archaeological Sources

Alexander, Jonathan & Paul Binski. *Age of Chivalry: Art in Plantagenet England 1200-1400*. London: Royal Academy of Arts 1987

Atkin, M. & D. H. Evans. *Excavations in Norwich 1971-1978*. Norwich: East Anglian Archaeology 1985

Biddle, Martin, Ian H. Goodall, & David A. Hinton *Object and Economy in Medieval Winchester (Winchester Studies 7.ii), vol. i and ii*. Oxford: Oxford University Press 1990

Burckhardt, Monica. *Mobilier Moyen-Age, Renaissance*. Paris: Charles Massin 1990

Chinnery, Vicot. *Oak Furniture: the British Tradition*. Woodbridge: Antique Collectors' Club 1988

Cowgill, J., M. de Neergaard, & N. Griffiths. *Knives and Scabbards*. London: Her Majesty's Stationery Office 1987

Crowfoot, Elizabeth, Frances Pritchard, & Kay Staniland. *Textiles and Clothing 1150-1450*. London: Her Majesty's Stationery Office 1992

Cunliffe, Barry. *Excavations at Portchester Castle, vols. 3 & 4*. New York: Thames and Hudson 1977

Eames, Penelope. *Furniture in England, France and the Netherlands from the Twelfth to the Fifteenth Century*. London: Furniture History Society 1977

Egan, Geoff. *Dress Accessories c. 1150 - c. 1450*. London: The Stationery Office 1991

Egan, Geoff. *The Medieval Household: Daily Living c.1150-c.1450*. London: The Stationery Office 1998

Grew, Frances & Margrethe de Neergaard. *Shoes and Pattens*. London: Her Majesty's Stationery Office 1988

Haslam, Jeremy. *Medieval Pottery*. Princes Risborough: Shire 1984

Husband, T. B. & J. Hayward. *The Secular Spirit: Life and Art at the End of the Middle Ages*. New York: Dutton 1975

Margeson, Sue et al. *Norwich Households*. Norwich: East Anglian Archaeology 1993

McCarty, Michael R. & Catherine M. Brooks. *Medieval Pottery in Britain AD 900-1600*. London: Leicester University Press 1988

Some Recipes from the Medieval Kitchen

Macrows

Take and make a thynne foyle of dowh, and kerve it on pieces, and cast hem on boilling water & seth it wele; take chese and grate it and butter cast bynethen and above as losyns, and serve forth

Macaroni: Take and make a thin sheet of dough, and carve it into pieces, and put them in boiling water and boil them well; take cheese and grate it and put butter (and cheese) beneath and above as for lozenges (lasagne), and serve forth.

Chykens in Dochee

Take chykenns and scald hem. Take parsel and sawge without eny other erbes. Take garlec and grapes and stoppe the chikens ful, and seeth hem in good broth so that they may esely be boyled thereinne. Messe hem and cast thereto powdor douce.

Chicken in Hotchpot: Take chickens and scald them. Take parsley and sage without any other herbs. Take garlic and grapes and stuff the chickens full and boil them in good broth so that they may easily be boiled within. Divide them into servings and sprinkle sweet powder (mixed spices) over them.

Blank-Mang

Take capons and seeth hem. Thenne take hem up. Take almandes blanced. Grynd hem and alay hem up with the same broth. Cast the mylk in a pot. Waisshe rys and do thereto and lat it seeth. Thanne take brawn of capons. Teere it small and do thereto. Take white Greece, sugar, and salt, and cast thereinne. Lat it seeth. Thene mess it forth and florish it with aneys in confitrede pther whyte and with almondes fryed in oil and serve it forth.

White-Dish: Take capons and boil them. Then take them out of the pot. Take blanched almonds. Grind them and mix them up with the same broth. Cast the [almond] milk in a pot. Wash rice and put it in the pot and let it boil. Then take meat of capons. Tear it small and put it in the pot. Take lard, sugar, and salt, and put them in the pot. Let it boil. Then divide it into servings and decorate it with red or white candied aniseed and with almonds fried in oil and serve it forth.